THE AUTHOR

THE GREAT WAR IN WEST AFRICA

BRIGADIER GENERAL E. HOWARD GORGES

C.B., C.B.E., D.S.O.

OFFICIER DE LA LÉGION D'HONNEUR ,
LATE THE MANCHESTER REGIMENT, AND
COMMANDANT WEST AFRICAN REGIMENT 1914-16

WITH FRONTISPIECE, 191 OTHER ILLUSTRATIONS
AND 15 MAPS

The Naval & Military Press Ltd

❖

Reproduced by kind permission of the Central Library,
Royal Military Academy, Sandhurst

Published by

The Naval & Military Press Ltd

Unit 10, Ridgewood Industrial Park,

Uckfield, East Sussex,

TN22 5QE England

Tel: +44 (0) 1825 749494

Fax: +44 (0) 1825 765701

www.naval–military-press.com

© The Naval & Military Press Ltd 2004

Printed and bound by Antony Rowe Ltd, Eastbourne

CONTENTS

CHAPTER VI

CHAPTER VII

CHAPTER VIII

CHAPTER IX

CHAPTER X

CHAPTER XI

CONTENTS

CHAPTER XII

APPENDICES

LIST OF ILLUSTRATIONS

FOREWORD

THIS account of the conquest of the Cameroons is a well-merited tribute to the West African native soldier and to the British officers who trained him in time of peace and who led him successfully during many months of active service under circumstances of great difficulty, inherent in the nature of the country and the deadly and depressing climate of the African Bush.

Among the more decisive and extensive operations in theatres of war in Europe, Egypt, and Palestine, these smaller " side shows " in Tropical Africa do not occupy a large place in the minds of our countrymen, and indeed are but little known by them save in the broadest outline.

They deserve, however, a detailed record in justice to the West African native soldier, who throughout the War upheld with tenacity, loyalty, and courage the honour of the Flag.

This record is all the more timely inasmuch as the West African Regiment, a fine regiment of twelve companies of which the author was Commandant at the time of the outbreak of war, and which took its full share in the Cameroon Expedition, has now been disbanded.

Nor should the record be lost of the many thousands of native carriers who alone made it possible for the columns to operate in the tangle of the African Bush far from the bases.

Few officers could be better qualified than General Gorges to write this book, owing to his intimate knowledge of Africa, east, west, north, and south, and of the African native soldier, his capacities, his limitations, his loyalty and endurance.

In General Gorges the native soldier has found a worthy chronicler.

J. F. DANIELL,

G.O.C. Sierra Leone, 1914–16.

PREFACE

HEREIN will be found a short narrative of the naval and military operations in Togoland and the Cameroons 1914–16. The Togoland adventure was skilfully and speedily accomplished, whilst the campaign in the Cameroons was a toilsome business of nineteen months' duration, resulting in the occupation by the Allies in the spring of 1916 of a vast and interesting block of Tropical Africa. Few people unconnected with the West Coast of Africa had ever heard of the Cameroons before the year 1914, and we hear of one old lady who when told that a certain officer was in the Cameroons expressed a pious hope that he liked the regiment and would not catch a cold from wearing a kilt !

While it is hoped that the narrative may prove of interest, especially to officers who have served and are now serving with African troops, in no sense is it put forward as a detailed account of the West African campaigns of the Great War or as being comparable to the more elaborate official history which will, no doubt, be published in due course. My chief aim and object in attempting to write up some of the happenings " coastwise " during the great upheaval—and I trust it is not now too late in the day—is to record the deeds of arms of our West African soldiers from Sierra Leone, Nigeria, Gold Coast, and Gambia, who, drawn into a contest of which their understanding was imperfect, yet kept the flag flying and game to the last, followed their officers through swamps, primeval forests, vast tracts of bush and elephant grass, over great mountain ranges and fighting, fell, believing in the greatness of England. I take pleasure also in recording the courage, endurance, and soldierly bearing of the French *tirailleurs*, Senegalais who fought side by side with our own black troops and shared with them the honours of war.

In addition to the African troops, the names of two other regiments should be mentioned for valuable services rendered in the later stages of the campaign, viz. the 5th Indian Light Infantry and half a battalion of the West India Regiment.

I have tried not to stress unduly the hardships of this " side-scene " of the War, and though the Germans fought with great courage and determination in defence of their colonies, the climate of the coast and low-lying regions of the interior was the arch-enemy causing many more casualties than bullets, for while tropical ulcers, dysentery, pneumonia, and rheumatism thinned the ranks of the native troops and transport carriers, malarial fevers played havoc with the Europeans.

> " Who'll shake his hand ? "
> " I," said the Fever,
> " And I'm no deceiver,
> I'll shake his hand ! "
>
> *Kipling.*

But the Medical Memoir tells the story.

ACKNOWLEDGMENTS

FIRST and foremost, I am indebted to Admiral Sir Cyril Fuller, K.C.B., C.M.G., D.S.O., R.N., the Commanding Officer of H.M.S. *Cumberland* and Senior Naval Officer at Duala during the campaign, for valuable and interesting information dealing with the naval operations in the Bight of Biafra ; to Captain F. Q. Champness, D.S.O., R.N., for granting me permission to take a few " tit-bits " from his captivating article " Doing Her Bit, an account of a Cruiser's operations in the Cameroons," and to the Editor of *Blackwood's Magazine*, in which the said article was published.

It gives me pleasure to acknowledge the help I have received from the following officers for placing at my disposal articles, papers, diaries, records, anecdotes, sketches and photographs connected with sailoring, soldiering and life on the Coast, both in pre-war and the fighting days : Surgeon H. C. A. Tandy-Cannon, who served on board H.M.S. *Challenger* during the naval operations ; Lieut. Colonel J. P. Law, D.S.O., Devonshire Regiment ; Lieut. Colonel B. G. Atkin, D.S.O., M.C., The Manchester Regiment ; Major C. S. Burt, D.S.O., South Staffordshire Regiment ; Lieut. Colonel H. R. H. Crawford ; Brevet Major S. J. Cole, O.B.E., Prince of Wales Volunteers ; Colonel J. C. B. Statham, C.M.G., C.B.E., R.A.M.C., and the late Captain C. J. Maclaverty. Then I have to thank the Manager of *The Times* Publishing Company Limited, for permission to make extracts and reproduce two sketch-maps from *The Times* History of the War ; the Manager, Illustrated Newspapers Limited, for some passages and sketches from the *Sphere ;* the Editor, *Windsor Magazine*, and Lady Johnston of St. John's Priory, Poling, for extracts from an article on the Cameroons by the late Sir Harry Johnston, G.C.M.G. ; the Secretary, Royal Geographical Society, and B. W. Fitch-Jones, Esq., for their courtesy in lending the photographs of the inscribed rock at Sierra Leone ; my old friend, Colonel J. R. Homfray, C.B.E., for his sketches of battle scenes, etc., and his son, Captain J. Homfray, M.C., Nigerian Civil Service, for graphically depicting " The Elements at Play." I would especially thank Lieut. Colonel C. S. Stooks, D.S.O., Indian Army, for allowing me to make free use of his interesting diary of the campaign ; the London Electrotype Agency Limited, and the Manager of the *Illustrated London News*, for kindly lending original drawings of battle scenes, etc.

Many photographs taken by Germans, and shown in the book, were found in the Colony during the progress of operations.

Finally, I wish to express my gratitude to Major General Sir John Daniell, K.C.M.G., General Officer Commanding at Sierra Leone, West Africa, during the War, for reading and correcting the manuscript and for writing a foreword.

E. H. G.

THE GREAT WAR IN
WEST AFRICA

CHAPTER I

IN the good old days before the Great War there
dwelt and flourished on the West African Coast a
very happy family in full enjoyment of the daily
round of "the piping times of peace."

There, on a beautiful wooded hill of eternal summer,
that juts into the broad Atlantic from the Colony of
Sierra Leone, it basked in the tropical sunshine. The
happy family was the West African Regiment and the
beautiful hill of eternal summer was Wilberforce, part of
the hill-station of Freetown and the Regimental Headquarters.

From the deck of an approaching vessel a panorama
of surpassing grandeur gradually reveals itself. Dark blue
ocean waters ripple into shady palm-fringed bays of
golden sands, the background of lofty forested hills display-
ing the most gorgeous ever-changing tints which pursue
the ever-changing lights. In a word, it is a scene to
which the pencil might perhaps do some justice, but
which defies all the powers of language adequately to
describe.

Sierra Leone, on account of its spacious natural harbour,
safe from the restless rollers of the Atlantic and its supply

of fresh water, was in ancient times much used by vessels sailing to the East by the Cape of Good Hope. Historically somewhat vague and sketchy, the earliest days of exploration would appear to go back to 500 B.C. by the Carthaginians ; then we hear of the Norman traders of A.D. 1346. Again in the year 1462, when the Portuguese navigators approached the harbour, the rumble of the thunder around the high peaks suggested to them the name of " Sierra Leone," the Lion Mountain, which the Colony now bears. Sir John Hawkins made no less than three voyages down this coast between 1562 and 1568, and in the latter year Thomas Cavendish on his voyage of circumnavigation spent several days in the harbour. Sir Francis Drake in the *Pelican* arrived there on the 22nd July, 1580, taking in food, water and cargo. He weighed again on the 24th July, arriving in England on 3rd November after a three years' world voyage toiling in the seas. During the Anglo-Dutch War of 1664–7, a Dutch fleet under Vice-Admiral de Ruyter visited the place and burnt the English factory on Tasso Island in the estuary of the Rokelle River above Freetown, and in this connection it is interesting to note that recently, during the course of some engineering work, a syenite boulder measuring some twenty by sixteen feet was dug up at King Jimmy Wharf, Freetown, and when completely excavated its surface was seen to be covered with many Dutch and English names, dates, etc. Amongst these names was that of Admiral de Ruyter.

In 1787 some hundreds of freed negro slaves who had been brought to England were transhipped and landed at Sierra Leone at the spot where Freetown now thrives. Subsequently more slaves came from America, and when slave ships were captured, the human cargoes were landed at Freetown and added to the population, and the Creoles of to-day are the descendants of this mixed slave population. In the year 1794 Freetown was sacked by

"PALM-FRINGED BAYS OF GOLDEN SANDS"

the French revolutionaries, who left the Colony practically in a state of destitution. Even in quite recent times this Colony was looked upon as one of the most deadly patches on God's earth where the white man, when he stepped ashore, abandoned all hope of returning to his native land, and still, in spite of vast improvements in the conditions of life and up-to-date methods of preventing and combating tropical diseases, it could scarcely be styled a health resort ; for interspersed with its sylvan hills are great hollows containing pestilential oozing swamps from which are drawn by the fierce rays of the African sun foul malarious mists, out of which myriads of mosquitoes and other insect pests are wafted on the evening breezes into the abodes of men, where they buzz and drone and chirp and sting and keep their revels by night. It is during these insectile carousals that the seeds of malaria are sown in men's bodies which, after a time, begin to wear them down and sap their manhood, causing some, after a short spell of coast life, visibly to degenerate. They become irritable and at times quite unapproachcble. " Old Harry " seems to possess their souls, for they refuse to sit at breakfast until they have " had it out " with the first unfortunate who happens to be wearing a cheerful countenance. Such are the effects of this climate ; but the climate must not be altogether blamed, especially in the case of those who cannot stand up against difficulties or steer clear of the temptations, chiefly drink and what is known on the Coast as the *Mammy Palaver*. These soon begin to tell upon those who give way to them, and then the climate steps in and gives the knock-out blow— and gets more than its fair share of the blame. But hard-drinkers were rare birds and though alcohol was more freely absorbed on the Coast than would have been the case in more temperate climes, I can say that during fifteen years service in Tropical Africa in peace and war, I never saw a British officer the worse for drink, and when one considers the depressing effect of the climate of the beauty spots in which they were called upon to serve, one marvels at their temperate habits of life and one understands why the native soldiers looked up to them, followed them through all the strife and in the end triumphed over our enemies. As to the effects of the climate on Europeans in earlier days of settlement, we read that one, Major Ricketts of the Royal African Corps, who was appointed Lieutenant Governor of the Colony in November, 1828, had the unique experience of witnessing during a short period of service on the Coast, the arrival and death of no less

Courtesy of B. W. Fitch-Jones, Esq., and Secretary R.G.S.

PORTION OF THE INSCRIBED ROCK SHOWING ADMIRAL DE RUYTER'S INSCRIPTION

than five Governors, viz. Governors MacCarthy, Turner, Campbell, Denham, and Lumley. Yet notwithstanding many discomforts and drawbacks, most of us managed to enjoy our tour of service on the Coast. We had every form of sport including tennis, cricket, racquets, excellent sea fishing, and good big-game shooting in the Bush.

Freetown, the capital and principal port of the Colony on the left bank of the estuary of the Rokelle river, lies at the base of a range of conical-wooded hills of which " Sugar loaf " is the most prominent feature. The houses of the town stretching up the valleys and spurs of these hills present a very picturesque appearance from the harbour.

> " It is a goodly sight to see
> What Heaven hath done for this delicious land !
> What fruits of fragrance blush on every tree !
> What goodly prospects o'er the hills expand ! "
>
> *Childe Harold.*

Almost every house has its garden in which the delicious avocada pear, orange, citron, pomegranate, mango, pineapple, and various other fruits are grown. Ginger, pepper, arrowroot, sweet potatoes, ground nuts, kola nuts, and many other valuable products are capable of large cultivation, but the natives lead too perfectly an indolent life and have but to scratch the rich soil in patches to produce all the fruits of the earth.

It is a busy town, where everybody from highest to lowest trades. In fact, the entire population appear to spend the days in trying to " do each other down." From sunrise to sunset the town resembles a human beehive. Creoles, Syrians, Mandingoes, Fulahs, Mendis, Temnis, half-castes pass to and fro in kaleidoscopic procession bent upon the all-absorbing business of the marketing of their wares. Their excitable squeals and twitters are like the discordant sounds of an agitated aviary. One becomes spell-bound watching this moving, perspiring mass of black humanity clothed in every variety of cheap finery. Men in swallow-tails and toppers ; gentlemen in shorts, thick hose and bowlers ; knots of *Kru* boys with their superb muscular development of arms and shoulders from the perpetual plying of the heavy surf-boat oars, chanting rhythmical sea ditties whilst resting from their briny toils ; very dark " knuts " in blue lounge suits and straw hats (Sierra Leonian " *gennellum, sah !* "), turbaned Mahomedan traders in flowing white robes mingle with

FREETOWN FROM MOUNT AUREOLE.   BRITISH SQUADRON IN THE ESTUARY

Petty Pagan Chiefs on holiday from the hinterland in brilliant robes of rich design, some wearing medals as large as dinner plates, others amulets and feathered head-dresses, with an occasional group of smart West African soldiers in their picturesque red fezes exchanging the glad eye with dusky damsels ; strolling players with weird musical instruments giving forth cinder-sifting sounds ; bare-legged women in velvet gowns, showy Manchester prints, and carpet slippers with marvellously shingled hair ; huge *Mammies* with their *piccins* (babies) tied to their backs. There they go, chanting, humming, shouting, quarrelling, and laughing—a delightfully human picture.

Well ! This is Freetown—free and safe and fair to all who pass within view of the Union Jack over Government House, which is set in the midst of this happy black life.

Writing of weird costumes reminds me of a little story I once heard when serving on the Coast. Passenger ships arriving in the harbours are boarded by black Custom House officials, their uniform not unlike that of an admiral. A certain ship coming to its anchorage had amongst its passengers an old Manchester merchant combining business with a pleasure trip down the Coast. When he appeared on deck his attention was arrested by one of these officials, who was behaving as though he had bought the ship.

" Who's that fellow ? " he inquired of one of the ship's officers.

" Couldn't say," replied the officer, " but he'll no doubt tell you if you ask him. They all speak ' trade ' English."

The merchant thereupon walked up to the brass-bound one, and taking hold of the lapel of his coat, said :

" I've been wondering who you are when you're at home."

" Sar, I am the Custom House," he replied, with some dignity. " And who may you be ? "

" Me ? " laughed the old Lancashire man. " Oh, I'm the cottage by the sea ! "

But a description of Freetown would be incomplete without a reference to its wonderful cotton tree—a marvel of stateliness towering above the centre of the town, a noble specimen of arboreal beauty. Were not all the grand *Palavers* of the Coast held under the soothing shade

REGENT STREET, FREETOWN

of its mighty, spreading branches ? Is not Cotton Tree Railway Station built hard by its gnarled buttresses ? Do not hosts of stinging red ants drop from its shimmering leaves and bury their powerful mandibles in the shiny necks of wily natives ? The answer in each case is in the affirmative.

The West African Regiment (W.A.R.), the only Imperial Native Corps in Africa administered by the War Office, was in pre-war days composed of some 60 British officers, 25 British non-commissioned officers, and 1500

West African soldiers recruited from various Pagan and
Mahomedan tribes in the Sierra Leone Protectorate—a
fine body of disciplined black troops.   Intellectually
nothing to write home about, their brain-boxes might be
divided into two compartments, the first containing wool,
the second cunning.   Yet if taken in the right way and
treated with firmness, patience, a dash of kindness, and,
above all, justice, they could be turned into good soldiers.
Cheerful, obedient, eager to learn and to please, they were,
in spite of many little human failings, thoroughly good
fellows.   The men enlisted from pagan tribes (Mendis and
Temnis), though possessing many soldierly qualities, were
prone to excitability, and were therefore at times difficult
to handle and control under sustained fire in " hot "
corners of the Bush, but the Mahomedan soldiers of the
regiment were of excellent fighting material and considered themselves superior to their pagan comrades,
whose throats, with little encouragement, they might be
disposed to slit in the name of Allah, and they went forth
to battle buoyed up with comforting words from Chapter 4
of the Koran :

   " Whosoever fighteth for the religion of God, whether
   he be slain or be victorious, we will surely give him a
   great reward."

Doubtless the West African soldier, like his white
prototype at home, did many things he ought not to have
done, but two things he did not do—he neither wore boots
nor ate Tommy's rations.   He went bare-footed at all
times, and was paid threepence a day, with which he
provided his own rations or " chop " as he called it.
Though a plain-living person, he would sometimes spend
his pay in the regimental canteen on such luxuries as
sardines and jam (" proper white-man chop "), but a
bowl of native rice mixed with a little dried shark,
flavoured with palm-oil and a few chillies, was his staple
food day in and day out, and it was surprising what hard

work he could perform on this simple fare. Indeed, as far as the Mendi was concerned, the ration problem was easily solved, for he was fond of lizards, partial to cats, and did not even shy at snakes. His marching powers were wonderful. With rifle, bandolier ammunition, blanket, and *machete* or native axe, he would march all day and all night too, if necessary. An hour or two to cook and eat his frugal meal, he would cover thirty-five to forty miles in the twenty-four hours with little effort, and in emergency even greater distances. Being bare-footed, he moved silently through the dense under-growth. He was not what you would call a " Bisley " shot, but as he had to fight in dense bush or forest, his method was to creep silently along and pot his adversary at short range without being seen or heard, and a very sound idea, too, for with good discipline and training he proved himself a nasty customer to tackle in his own element. The Bush in places was impenetrable

THE COTTON TREE

except to these Africans, who with their *machetes* could work their way through with great rapidity and skill.

Some years ago a new general officer was appointed to command the troops in Sierra Leone, and one day he went forth to inspect some companies of the regiment practising " Bush fighting," and ran into a young sub-altern, who was walking along a narrow Bush pathway alone. The General stopped him and asked him what he was doing, and the subaltern said :

" I'm doing company training, sir."

To which the General replied : " I am aware that you

c

THE WEST AFRICAN REGIMENT (POST-WAR)

Courtesy of Lisk Carew.

should be, but I want to know what you are doing alone in the Bush when you should be training your men ? "

Whereupon the subaltern blew a shrill blast on his whistle, and in a few seconds a company of grinning and perspiring West African soldiers in full war paint sprang from the undergrowth on either side of the pathway. The General hastily apologised, smiled, and moved on.

It is interesting to note that the regimental march of the W.A.R. was "Rule, Britannia," and being anxious to learn how an African native corps could have come by this tune for its march, I once asked the native Regimental Sergeant Major if he could enlighten me on the subject. He replied :

" Yes, sah. Black soldier very good Briton. Briton nebber nebber slave."

That put the lid on it !

The rôle of the regiment was the defence of the Sierra

Courtesy of Lisk Carew.

SOME N.C.O.'S WEST AFRICAN REGIMENT

Leone Colony, though in emergency it was liable for service overseas.

Beyond a certain amount of scrapping against ill-armed and undisciplined recalcitrant tribes in the hinterland, the men had not seen war. They had not tasted the glamour and display or endured the hardships and sufferings of modern warfare, and little did they comprehend in that quiet and peaceful month of July 1914 that they were destined soon to have their fill of excitement, toil, fevers, wounds, and pain. So too with the officers. Few had felt the fever of the " Field " or known the risk of disaster, the elation of victory ; the anguish of the strife, which, added to other passions, constitute a strain which some human nerves are unable very long to endure.

We were fortunate in having at that time as General Officer commanding the troops in West Africa Major General J. F. Daniell, Royal Marine Light Infantry,[1] a firm, kind and considerate Commander with a shrewd and kindly insight into the heart of human nature ; he inspired confidence in his officers which soon ripened into friendship and regard. As Commandant of the West African Regiment, it was my privilege and pleasure to serve under him previous to and after the declaration of war, and to have been intimately associated with him in the early preparations for the defence of the Colony. Is was well indeed that an officer of his rank and reputation happened to be on the spot, for as the struggle developed and spread to all parts of the African continent, the place acquired much importance as a naval coaling station, possessing as it did the finest harbour on the Coast. As the enemy submarine activity extended it became the rendezvous for all homeward-bound ships from African ports. Here under the guns of the fortress the transports could assemble and ride safely at anchor awaiting their turn to join the convoys under escort of H.M. warships. Moreover, Sierra Leone became a supply depôt for the Expeditionary Forces operating against the German Colonies in Africa. Reinforcements, wastage drafts, ammunition, ordnance stores of every description, food and thousands of transport carriers, without which the expeditions could never have existed—all these were provided from Sierra Leone under the personal super-vision of General Daniell, whose chief staff officer was

[1] Now Major General Sir John Daniell, K.C.M.G.

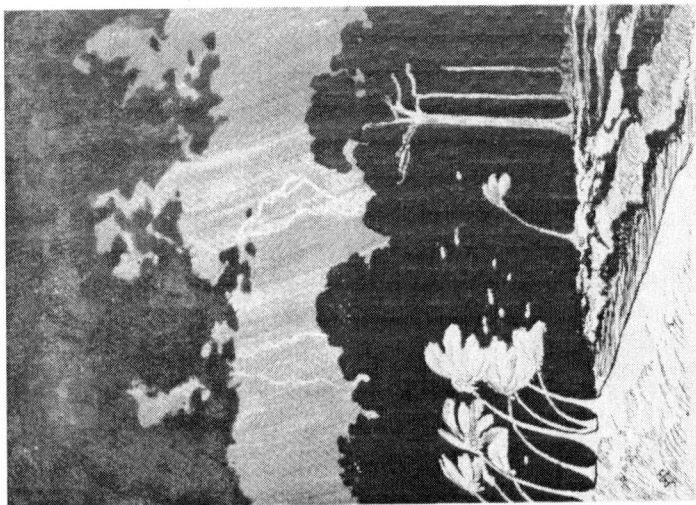

"MILKIES" HURLED THROUGH SPACE

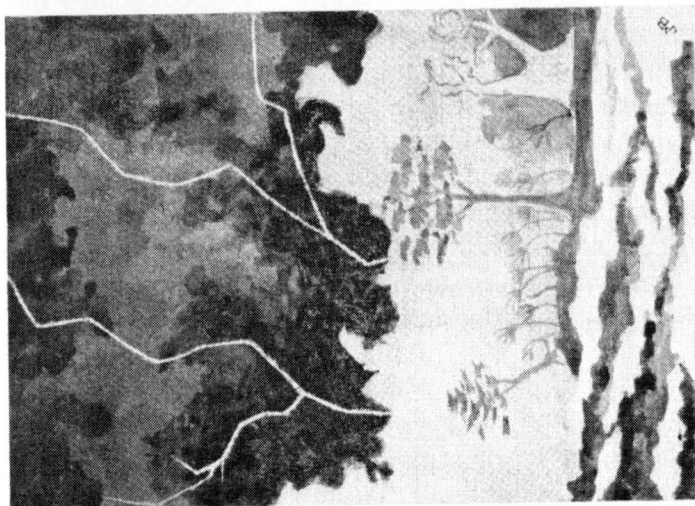

THE ELEMENTS AT PLAY

Major, now Brigadier General, Bonham Faunce, C.B.E., an officer with unique experience of the Coast and its many peculiarities.

At the time of which I write we were well into the rainy season, which sets in about May and dies away in October. This dismal period is made still more depressing by a succession of violent storms known as tornadoes. Agitated sea-birds, with mournful shrieks and mewings, forecast a pause in heaven's holiday of calm and sunshine, while leaden storm-clouds foregather to form a great canopy over the land and seaward almost to the horizon. The atmosphere is in a restless mood, and fitful gusts of moaning wind accompany heavy spots of warm rain. Then a momentary calm followed by increasing strength of swirling winds and heavy showers, and finally, the fury of the storm. The canopy is torn to shreds and heaven smites with an open hand, lashing the ocean into mountainous waves, uprooting trees wholesale, and lifting roofs from houses ; stately coco-nut palms bend and bow their heads to the very ground, while the " milkies " are hurled into space as from giant catapults. The floodgates of the firmament are opened and sheets of hissing rain deluge the valleys, transforming meandering brooks into boiling rivers, while lightnings fall in great forked splashes and Thor's hammer splits the mountains. Destruction is dealt out broadcast by these mighty elemental convulsions, and then—a sudden calm, as though all the heavenly orders had become exhausted, following a display of Atlantean stunts which fortunately for all living things in those regions are infrequent and of short duration.

It was during one of these upheavals at about the cheerless hour of 3 a.m. on 30th July, 1914, I was lying restlessly on my camp bed, very wideawake and wondering if the roof would hold, that I received an unexpected visit from the Regimental Adjutant, who had braved the elements to say that the order to mobilise had been cabled from the War Office. Realising what that meant, we made our way to the office and there unearthed the secret file, so clearly drawn up at Headquarters that before dawn on that eventful day the war machine in our little African corner was quietly set in motion. Life, somehow, changed from that hour—indeed, our very skins seemed to change ! We cast off the old and emerged in the new, fresh and keen to play our small part in the severest and most sanguinary struggle of the ages.

CHAPTER II

AT the outbreak of war, Sir E. M. Mereweather, K.C.V.O., C.M.G., was Governor and Commander-in-Chief of the Colony and Protectorate, and, as previously stated, Major General J. F. Daniell commanded the Troops with the following staff :—

Aide-de-Camp : Captain H. W. Roberts, R.A. General Staff Officer, 2nd grade : Major B. Faunce, W.I.R. Dep. Asst. Adjt. and Qr.-Mr. Gen. : Major M. H. C. Bird, R.A. Officer Commanding Royal Artillery : Lieut. Col. R. G. Merriman, D.S.O., R.G.A. Officer Commanding Royal Engineers : Major C. B. Bonham, R.E. Officer Commanding Army Service Corps : Major A. W. Johns, A.S.C. Senior Medical Officer : Colonel J. J. Gerrard, M.B. Chief Ordnance Officer : Major C. T. Fisher, A.Ord.Dept. Command Paymaster : Major J. C. Hewett, A.P.Dept.

The Imperial Garrison for the Defence of the Fortress consisted of :—

No. 50 Company Royal Garrison Artillery (British). The Sierra Leone Company Royal Garrison Artillery (Native). No. 36 Fortress Company, Royal Engineers (British). 1st Battalion West India Regiment. The West African Regiment. Detachments Royal Army Medical

Corps, Royal Army Ordnance Corps, Royal Army Service Corps.

In the Protectorate, quartered at Daru, on the railway, was a battalion of the West African Frontier Force, known as the Sierra Leone Battalion and administered by the Colonial Office.

The British officers of the Garrison and most of the troops were located in good quarters and barracks, perched on the hills overlooking Freetown. The Gunners and Engineers on Tower Hill, the West India Regiment on Mount Aureole, and the West Africans at Wilberforce, where cool night breezes wafted in from the ocean gave refreshing sleep to dog-weary souls. The official residence of the General Commanding was at Hill Station, but the Headquarter offices were almost adjoining Government House in Freetown. Hill Station, some 800 feet above sea-level, was connected with Freetown by a light hill railway, known as the mountain section of the

Courtesy of Lisk Carew.

SIERRA LEONE RAILWAY,
MOUNTAIN SECTION

Sierra Leone railway and said to be the steepest non-funicular railway in existence, its maximum gradient being 1 in 22. As the toy train panted and puffed its tortuous way to its lofty terminus, a picturesque panorama of green-clad hills and river gorges with falls of flashing silver was presented to the passenger, with an occasional peep at the Atlantic. The majority of the Government officials also dwelt in comfortable bungalows in Hill Station, from whence they proceeded daily to their work in the town.

The Sierra Leone main line railway starting from

Freetown ran through the heart of the Protectorate to Pendembu, over 200 miles, with a branch line from Boia to Baga (115 miles). It was of narrow gauge, $2\frac{1}{2}$ feet, and said to be one of the slowest lines on earth !

The Fortress armament consisted of fixed defence guns and mobile artillery, and without disclosing official secrets, one might venture to hazard the remark " sufficient to give a warm reception to hostile craft approaching within effective range." The fixed defences were manned

SIERRA LEONE MOUNTAIN BATTERY MARCHING PAST, CARRYING GUNS, LIMBERS, WHEELS, AMMUNITION, ETC., ON THEIR HEADS

by the British and the movable artillery by the native gunners. The searchlights were worked by the Fortress Company Royal Engineers.

Included in the mobile artillery was a battery of 2.95 M.M. Hotchkiss quick-firing mountain guns, a most useful, effective and handy little weapon for fighting in African forest and hill country ; a great support to our Native Infantry, and the weapon that perhaps did more than anything else to " chatter the ivories " of the German native soldiers. When dismounted, the gun makes up into some ten loads, the various component parts being carried on the heads of the gun-carriers, fine, stalwart, active fellows. Many a time have I watched them and the native gunners, led by their officers after long tiring marches, weary and footsore but without a murmur, mounting and bringing the guns into action with surprising speed and skill.

Concerning the infantry of the Garrison, the West India Regiment, as its name implies, drew its recruits from the West Indian Islands. Its Headquarters and

Courtesy of Lisk Carew.

THE WEST INDIA REGIMENT IN PICTURESQUE ZOUAVE DRESS

depôt were at Jamaica. The West Indian soldier was endowed with a higher intellect than the West African, and many of the men were well educated and intelligent, making first-class signallers and telephone operators. They were also well-disciplined, staunch troops and good shots. In pre-war days there were two battalions, one of which was quartered in Jamaica, the other in Sierra Leone, exchanging stations biennially. This famous corps, after a century and a half of distinguished record, was disbanded at Jamaica in 1926 at a most impressive and touching ceremony. On its colours it bore a long list of battle honours, including Dominica, Martinique,

Courtesy of Lisk Carew.

THE WEST AFRICAN REGIMENT (PRE-WAR)

Guadaloupe, Ashantee 1873–4, West Africa 1887, 1892–3–4, Sierra Leone 1898, and in the Great War the campaigns of the two battalions were, with one exception, confined to the continent which for so many years had been the chief scene of their honourable services. Both in East and West Africa they won fresh laurels, and when the War was ended, besides Palestine 1918, the campaigns of East Africa 1916–18, Cameroons 1915–16, completed the list of their war honours. The first Battalion which was quartered in Sierra Leone in 1914 was commanded by a fine soldier and great sportsman, Colonel Hepworth Hill.

The West African Regiment had a twelve company organisation. In peace time, Headquarters and seven companies were stationed at Wilberforce, the remaining five at posts in the Protectorate stretching out northwards towards the frontier of French Guinea. At the outbreak of war these outpost companies were withdrawn to augment the garrison of the fortress.

At the time of which I write, there were serving with the regiment a keen and competent lot of officers, selected from British units for a tour of service on the Coast. Some were on home leave and on shooting expeditions in the hinterland, chasing Elephant, Bush cow and Bongo, and a few were on special service, such as Boundary Commissions, Survey and Intelligence work.

Major E. Vaughan (now Brigadier General E. Vaughan, C.M.G., D.S.O.) of my own regiment, the Manchesters, a popular and distinguished officer, was my acting second-in-command, and amongst others I would mention Major J. P. Law (now Lieut. Col. J. P. Law, D.S.O.) of the Devons, who later commanded a battalion of that renowned regiment, a good soldier, sportsman and naturalist, very keen in those days on collecting butterflies and known by the native soldiers

CAPTAINS WILLIAMS AND BRAND, WEST AFRICAN REGIMENT. (BOTH KILLED IN ACTION)

of the regiment as "*Dat Major who lib for hunt dem flutterbies.*" Major Frank Maude, an old school-fellow, and one of the best and kindest of men; Captains John Hodding (who had served for ten years with the regiment); A. C. Taylor (dear old Taylor), Cameronians; R. D. Keyworth, Oxford and Bucks L.I., our "Sunny Jim," for in good times and bad he ever had a cheery smile for all—a great asset on the Coast, a brave and good soldier too, beloved by officers and men alike (now Lieut. Col.); L. J. Robertson, D.S.O., Bedfords; Lieutenants B. G. Atkin, Manchesters (now Lieut. Col., D.S.O. and M.C.), C. S. S. Burt, D.S.O., South Staffords; H. J. Minnikin, M.C., West India Regiment; H. W.

Dakeyne, Royal Warwicks (now Lieut. Col. and D.S.O.) ; E. G. Redway, M.C., Royal Irish, affectionately nick-named " Monkey Redway," being a fine boxer and possessed of great strength and agility. Of those who fell gloriously in the Cameroons and on other Fields, I would mention Lieut. Col. A. G. Grant, second-in-command, who was on leave at the outbreak of war and was killed in Flanders leading his regiment to the attack ; Captain C. H. Dinnen, The King's Regiment, my former Adjutant, Staff Captain and intimate friend, whose soldierly qualities and noble character deserve that his memory should be cherished with affection. An old campaigner, bearing many wounds and scars, he remained to the end a perfect enthusiast at his profession, and he now lies at rest beside two of his companions-in-arms in a sequestered vale in the heart of Africa. Then there was Lieutenant Jimmy Dimmer, who gained his commission from the ranks of the King's Royal Rifle Corps. Of dauntless courage, he won his V.C. in the retreat from Mons and was killed during the German onslaught of March 1918, having risen from subaltern to Lieutenant Colonel within the span of four years. Captains E. S. Brand, Royal Fusiliers ; F. T. Williams, Northamptons ; W. S. Rich, Cheshires ; B. J. Thruston, Lincolns ; W. F. G. Willes, Dorsets, and many more loyal, brave and true-hearted brother officers who were serving with the regiment in those far-off peaceful times.

In conformity with the post-war policy of reducing Colonial establishments, the West African Regiment was also disbanded in June 1928. Its formation synchronised with that of the Sierra Leone Protectorate in 1896. Though short-lived, it served a useful purpose, taking part in many expeditions up and down the Coast. On its colours it bore the following battle honours :—" Sierra Leone 1897–98 "—" Ashanti 1900 "—" Cameroons 1914–16 "—" Duala." H.R.H. The Prince of Wales was its Colonel-in-Chief.

Such was the Garrison of Sierra Leone where in the years immediately preceding the War there occurred mild outbreaks of a nervous type of disorder which may be appropriately styled " Hungitis." The annual training and manœuvres were worked out with the sole object of repelling German raids, the " idea " being that transports packed with German (European) troops, equipped to the last button, escorted by ships of war, appeared suddenly off some point on the Coast beyond the range of the Fortress guns, that after this force had disembarked, completed its goose-stepping on the beach and chanted its hymn of hate, it was to be drawn inland and, in a conveniently prepared Golgotha, ambushed and wiped out. On paper, an easy operation for the defenders, but with a small garrison of black troops and a handful of Europeans, the latter tied to the fixed armament, in practice difficult to accomplish. And so as time passed the German Bogey haunted us by day and danced on our chests at night.

CAPTAIN C. S. BURT, D.S.O., WEST AFRICAN REGIMENT, WITH CADDIE ON WILBERFORCE GOLF LINKS

This last ditch business, this passive parapet policy, naturally tended to destroy the offensive spirit. We knew of no schemes prepared for the despatch of an Expeditionary Force to invade German territories in Africa. Such adventures were undreamed of in those halcyon days. Consequently we dug ourselves in furiously to start with, and when there was no more digging to be done, and every officer and soldier knew exactly what to do and how to do it, we settled down according to plan to defend the Colony against the hated enemy, awaiting with patience and fortitude the day of his coming.

The mobilisation arrangements worked admirably and smoothly, as indeed they were bound to do, with no enemy to disturb them. But as time passed and the submarine cable gave forth its daily bulletin of the stupendous events then following each other in rapid succession by land and sea, a certain restlessness of mind began to assert itself in the garrison. A desire to get on to the canvas of this great world picture. A frame of mind excusable perhaps, in the circumstances, and especially so in the case of those junior officers who, possessed of boundless ambition and craving for distinction, beheld the chance of a lifetime, their young hearts beating high to tread the path of glory and above all to fight for England, the land of beauty, valour, and truth !

Dulce bellum inexpertis.

But on reflection, and in calmer moments, it was realised that a proportion of officers must of necessity remain with the Native troops—that if all those then serving on the Coast went to Europe, others would have to be sent out to replace them—that it resolved itself into a question of luck. Even as it was, the regiments were seriously depleted of their officers, the War Office having ordered most of those on leave when war was declared to rejoin their British units.

At last, towards the end of August 1914, a ray of hope illumined the Peninsula. Future expeditions were foreshadowed, though in nebulous form. Rumour ran riot, until finally it leaked out that troops from the Protectorate were actually being shipped overseas.[1] And then a calmer atmosphere pervaded the ante-rooms of the various garrison and regimental messes.

The Coast dialect was at times most bewildering and almost as difficult to understand as the vernacular ; for instance, if one called one's servant and the reply came,

[1] On 23rd August, 1914, two companies of the Sierra Leone Battalion West African Frontier Force were despatched as a reinforcement to Togoland.

" *Sah, I lib for chop*," it was to be understood he was having a meal and couldn't for the moment be disturbed ! For a bad smell they would say " *'trong niff-niff too big.*" A conceited young gentleman would be known as " *Bwoy head big too much.*" Sierra Leone to them is *Sally Own.* And many other queer expressions used in the ordinary course of conversation by the more uneducated classes could be given. The conversation and writings of the better educated savoured more of the quaint and entertaining phraseology of the Indian Babu. As an illustration,

THE COMMANDANT'S BUNGALOW AND NATIVE LINES, WILBERFORCE

a letter is here given ; it is a request from a Creole gentleman for the band of the West African Regiment to perform at local entertainments. Very friendly, plausible, with a little flattery thrown in, it runs :—

Sir,

Only this night was I in receipt of your letter communicating the regrettable information that the Commandant and officers of the W.A.R. could not allow their band to play at the Wilberforce Maze.

I trust you will kindly pardon the liberty I am now respectfully asking to be permitted to state that I very much regret certain representations made which

D

were far from being the whole truth, but upon which you had no alternative assuming to be correct, to come to the above unfortunate decision.

Since the founding of this modest retreat one of my greatest difficulties was the securing of music. On occasions I have had the services of a few so-called instrumentalists from Freetown to perform. It has, however, happened that the public having been regaled with one set of pieces *ad nauseum* had been quite surfeited. Though not financially strong, but to meet the require- ments of a fastidious public resorting to the Maze, I felt it incumbent, if the prestige of this juvenile but rising Institution has to be maintained, I have not to be in- different to the just and respectful request made, but unselfishly contribute my all to the upbuilding of this abode of fun in which interest increases daily.

My friends and I have on rare occasions been enraptured with the melodious strains of your harmonious band which under abnormal conditions it is but vain to expect.

Relying therefore on the kind and sympathetic aid which I respectfully crave at the hands of the Commandant and officers of so distinguished a regiment, I have the honour to beg your most favourable recommendation of my application, and grant to me, dear gentlemen, the help I imploringly supplicate.

Remaining with honour,

Your obedient Servant,

He had his band !

Immediately after the outbreak of war, the Government had under consideration operations against the German oversea possessions, and with regard to West Africa it was decided to make the high-power wireless telegraph station at Kamina in Togoland the first objective. This installa- tion was one of the most powerful then in existence, being able to communicate direct with Berlin, South-West

Africa, and German East Africa, thus forming a vital link in the enemy's scheme of communications.

Togoland was acquired by Germany in 1884, being among the firstfruits of the partition of Africa among European Powers, a partition which resulted from H. M. Stanley's discovery of the course of the Congo and his revelation of the abundant richness of the interior of the equatorial regions of the continent. Togoland, part of the old slave coast of West Africa, has only 32 miles of seaboard, and though its hinterland widens, its total area is less than 34,000 square miles — about the size of Ireland. When the Germans entered into the scramble for Africa, Togo was the sole patch of coast in Upper Guinea not appropriated by other European States, and it was hemmed in, save seawards, by French and British territory. Dahomey on the east, the Gold Coast on the west, and the Upper Senegal and Niger Colony on the north. Differing in no essential

MAP OF TOGOLAND.

respect in physical features from the adjacent districts of the West Coast, Togoland is rich in sylvan products, and its resources had been greatly developed by German enterprise. Lome, the capital and chief port, a creation of the Fatherland, lies near the Gold Coast border.

It was considered probable that the occupation of this small German Colony would not present any very great difficulty, and on 5th August, 1914, orders were sent to the Gold Coast to prepare an Expeditionary Force to carry out the operations. At the same time it was decided that, in order to deliver an effective attack on the Cameroons, reinforcements both naval and military would be required, and that the initiation of offensive operations in that quarter should be deferred for the time being.

When the European situation became threatening in July 1914, Major von Döring, Acting Governor and Commander of the Troops in Togoland, made preparations to attack the French in Dahomey, on the assumption that Great Britain would not enter into the war. When he found out his error he abandoned his design. Acting on instructions from Berlin, in telegrams dated 4th and 5th August, addressed to M. William Ponty, Governor General of French West Africa, to the Lieutenant Governor of Dahomey and to the Governor of the Gold Coast, he proposed that Togoland and the neighbouring French and British Colonies should remain neutral. The German Government shortly afterwards came to have wider conceptions of neutrality in Equatorial Africa, conceptions to which reference is made later on, but the Togo proposal was a distinct move, and though reasons of humanity and the supposed need of the white races to present a solid front to the Blacks were urged by Major von Döring, the real object of the Germans in wishing to keep Togoland neutral was to preserve for their use the Kamina wireless station. Both the French and British authorities refused to entertain the proposal. The Lieutenant Governor of Dahomey, M. Charles Noufflard, who did not even answer Major von Döring's telegram, directed Commandant Maroix, the Senior Military Officer in Dahomey, to open hostilities. On 6th August French Colonial troops crossed the Togoland border near the coast. They met with no opposition ; Little Popo (Anecho) was seized, and on the evening of 8th August the town of Togo was occupied. On their side the Gold Coast authorities had not been idle. Mr. W. C. F. Robertson, Acting Governor, in the absence of Sir Hugh Clifford, and Captain F. C. Bryant, R.A., Senior Officer on the Gold Coast Station, took prompt and energetic measures. European volunteers at Accra, Sekondi, and Kumasi were enrolled, and every necessary step was taken both for defence and offence. On 6th August Captain Barker was sent to Lome under a flag of truce to demand the surrender of Togoland, and was told to point out to Major von Döring that, as strong columns were ready to invade the Colony from west, east, and north, his position was hopeless. A twenty-four hours' armistice was granted. When

GERMAN RECRUITS AT DRILL

Captain Barker returned to Lome at 6 p.m. on 7th August he found that the German troops had evacuated the town and that the District Commissioner left behind by Major von Döring had instructions to surrender the Colony as far as a line drawn 74 miles north of Lome. Major von Döring, the German troops, and many German civilians had retired up the railway, the Acting Governor having received imperative instructions to defend the wireless station at Kamina.

Up to this time the French and British authorities had worked independently, but on 8th August arrangements were made between Mr. Robertson and M. Noufflard for their co-operation. Captain Bryant, who was granted the temporary rank of Lieutenant Colonel, was in chief command of the allied forces. Captain Castaing, of the French Colonial Infantry, commanded the French column (8 Europeans and 150 Senegalese Tirailleurs) which, having completed the occupation of south-east Togoland, joined Colonel Bryant's troops on 18th August.

Colonel Bryant had landed at Lome on 12th August with two companies of the Gold Coast Regiment, machine-guns, medical transport, and supply staffs. The total strength of the British Force was 57 Europeans and 535 Natives, with 2000 carriers and labourers. Pushing up the railway towards Kamina, the main body came into contact with the enemy on 15th August. On the same day Captain Potter, with a company of the Gold Coast Regiment, very neatly trapped a much stronger column of the enemy operating on the railway at Agbelafoe, by placing himself between it and von Döring's force. By 20th August Colonel Bryant's column had marched to Nuatja, and on the 22nd there was a stubborn fight at the village of Chra. The enemy, whose force consisted of 60 Europeans and 400 Native soldiers and 3 machine-guns, held a very strong entrenched position north of the Chra river, the railway bridge over which had been blown up. The bush here was very dense, and the attacking columns were unable to keep touch with one another. After fighting all day the Allies failed to dislodge the enemy. At nightfall they entrenched themselves, prepared to renew the engagement at dawn, but during the night the Germans evacuated their position. Major von Döring had learned that another force, a French column under Commandant Maroix, advancing from the east, was within two days' march of Kamina, and he was unwilling to risk depletion of the garrison available for its defence.

At the Chra river fight the Germans suffered little loss, but the Anglo-French casualties were 78 (including 23 killed), or 17 per cent of the force engaged. The hottest fighting fell to the French column, which attacked the enemy's left, but after getting to within fifty yards of the trenches was forced to retire. Here Lieutenant Guillemart of the French Colonial Infantry and Lieutenant G. M. Thompson (Royal Scots, attached Gold Coast Regiment) were killed. Lieutenant Thompson had been placed in command of a company of Senegalese Tirailleurs ; after the fight he was found surrounded by the bodies of a Gold Coast Native non-commissioned officer and the sergeant, two corporals and nine privates of the

AIMING DRILL

Senegalese, who had died in his defence. The party was buried on the spot, Thompson's grave in the centre of the gallant group.

On the night of 24th-25th August loud explosions were heard at Colonel Bryant's camp in the direction cf Kamina, and in the morning the masts of the great wireless station, which had been clearly visible from the Allies' advanced post, were seen to have disappeared. The wireless station had, in fact, been destroyed by the enemy. There had been a good deal of dissension among the 200 Germans, military and civilian, gathered at Kamina, and Major von Döring, though amply supplied with arms and ammunition, abandoned his intention of resisting to the last. On 25th August he sent Major von Roben, his second-in-command, to Colonel Bryant, offering to surrender on terms, but von Roben was told that the surrender must be unconditional. To this von Döring agreed on the 26th, and on the next day Colonel Bryant took possession of Kamina. He had brought to a rapid conclusion a small campaign which, mishandled, might easily have been much prolonged, and his success was very largely due to his initiative and promptitude. For his services he was promoted to the substantive rank of Major and received the C.M.G.

While Colonel Bryant's operations were in progress, British and French columns occupied northern Togoland. The rapidity of the movements of the Allies completely surprised the Germans, who offered but a feeble resistance. Acting on instructions from Captain C. H. Armitage, Chief Commissioner of the Northern Territories, Major Marlow, with a party of eight men only, occupied Yendi, the German Commissioner being misled by spies into thinking that a large force was being brought against him. The rest of northern Togoland was seized by French forces numbering 630 rifles all told, under Captain Bouchez of the 2nd Regiment Senegalese Tirailleurs. Traversing an inundated region crossed by numerous unfordable rivers and under continuous rain, the French column covered 310 miles in 20 days. The German troops at Sansanne Mango, over 400 strong, fled before them, and on the second day of their retreat 180 of the German native soldiers deserted to the French, but this was typical of the attitude of the natives of Togoland to their German masters. Equally typical was the eagerness of the natives of the French and British Colonies to help in crushing the common enemy. A picturesque feature of Captain Bouchez's force was a body of Mossi warriors, inhabitants of a kingdom in the Niger Bend under French protection. They volunteered their services, each chieftain coming in feudal fashion to the rendezvous with his retainers in ful war paint. Colonel Bryant employed no partisans, but the chiefs and peoples of the Gold Coast and Ashanti were lavish in help. Besides much other financial assistance they defrayed the whole cost—£60,000—incurred in the British military operations, and also the cost of subsequent administration—£3000 a month. Major von Döring armed natives over whom he had no control and hundreds of them

AT THE GYM

were let loose in the Bush. However, the vast majority of the natives gave no trouble, and in a few weeks the economic life of the country was being carried on as smoothly as if there had been no interruption to it whatever.

It will thus be noted that the conquest of Togoland was a comparatively simple task, speedily and successfully completed. The beginning of the end, so to speak, of the German dream of a great African Empire.

CHAPTER III

THE purpose of this chapter is to give some idea of the nature of the country in which we were called upon to fight.

Cameroons, physically and geographically, is one of the most interesting portions of Africa. The name spelt incongruously in German, " Kamerun "—on the mistaken assumption that it was a native word—is derived from the Portuguese. When, towards the close of the fifteenth century, the Portuguese explorers sailed down the West African Coast they came—passing on the way a most notable mountain—to a great estuary, the river of the Duala people. This they called Rio dos Camaroes, or Shrimp river, from the abundance of large shrimps or small prawns found in its brackish waters. The Spanish version of the name—Camarones—was taken up by the English navigators, and by them converted into Cameroons. Possibly the Portuguese were preceded on the West Coast of Africa, as discoverers, by the Genoese. It is, at any rate, an attested fact that more than a hundred years before the Portuguese entered the Gulf of Guinea there was painted—probably at Genoa in 1351—the Laurentian Portolano, a map which gave the shape of the African continent with some approach to correctness of outline, and indicated the region where the Cameroon mountain rises abruptly from the sea-coast. The Portuguese obtained no foothold here, however. French, Dutch and English slave-traders frequented Ambas Bay and the

Cameroons or Duala delta, but the dominant people, the
Duala, were stalwart and warlike, and proved too strong

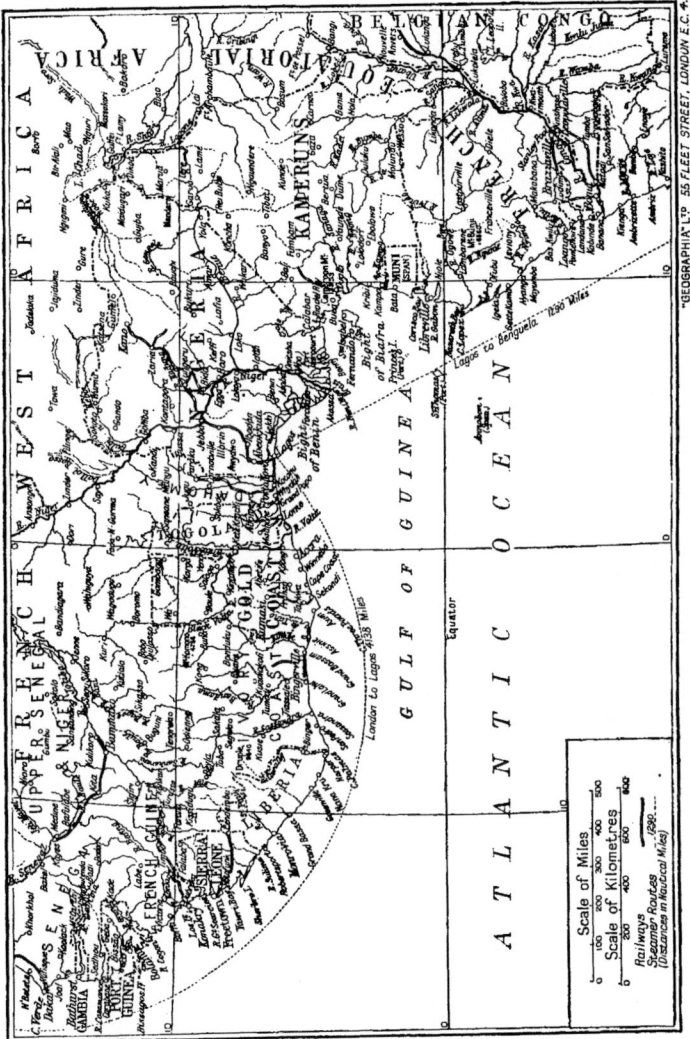

MAP SHOWING WEST COAST POSSESSIONS OF EUROPEAN POWERS
FROM CAPE VERDE TO CONGO

in their independence for any European Power to secure
a settlement. Indeed, on account of the truculence of the
natives, the hinterland remained a scarcely known region
until the middle of the nineteenth century. Trading

posts were established in and near the Cameroons estuary as early as the seventeenth century ; this trade, however, was confined to the coast, the Duala being recognised as intermediaries between the coast factories and the interior, whither they allowed no strange trader to proceed. In 1837 the King of Bimbia, a district on the mainland, on the north of the Duala estuary, made over a large part of the country round Ambas Bay to Great Britain. In 1845, at which time there was a flourishing trade in slaves between the Guinea Coast and America, the Baptist Missionary Society made its first settlement at Duala, that great missionary Alfred Saker obtaining from the Akwa family the site for a Mission station. In 1848 another station was established at Bimbia, and so as time went on Saker and his colleagues converted the Duala clans to real and permanent civilisation, winning them over by reason, by example, and by teaching useful trades and professions. Saker taught them to read and write and print their own tongues, to be good carpenters, brickmakers, and bricklayers. He made their lives busy and contented, and with the aid of British men-of-war the oversea slave trade was finally suppressed in 1875. In 1858, on the expulsion of the Baptists from the Island of Fernando Po, Saker founded in Ambas Bay a colony of the freed negroes, who then left the Island, the Settlement being named Victoria. Towards the close of the nineteenth century, after much peaceful penetration, chiefly by missionaries, various English and German firms had firmly established trading stations in the Cameroons and other rivers.

In 1884 Bismarck despatched Dr. Gustav Nachtigal to consolidate German interests in those regions. With commendable enterprise and audacity the Imperial Emissary concluded several hasty treaties with native chieftains and, hoisting the German flag at suitable points, proclaimed German protectorates first over Togoland and later, on 15th August, 1884, over the Cameroons.

Not long after the signature of this treaty the native chiefs
discovered that they had in the Teuton a master not to
their liking, and certain unpleasant incidents induced the
Germans to send a squadron, under Rear-Admiral Knorr,
to the Bight of Biafra. It was on board the *Bismarck*,
a vessel of this squadron, that
Admiral von Scheer, who commanded the German fleet at the
battle of Jutland, made his début
as a naval officer.

These hastily concluded treaties
apparently took the British Government of the day by surprise, and,
after prolonged negotiations, the
position was legalised by a treaty
signed in 1885, Germany agreeing
to renounce some shadowy claims
to territory at the mouth of the
Niger, while in return Great Britain
waived her prior rights with regard
to Dr. Nachtigal's acquisitions.

In 1911 the Agadir incident
occurred, when the Germans appeared to challenge in the most
deliberate manner the claims of
France to supremacy in Morocco,
and brought Europe to the verge
of war. At first Germany demanded in return for her recogni-
tion of a French protectorate in

NATIVE GENTLEMAN OF
LOMIE

Morocco the cession to her of the major part of French
Equatorial Africa, including the whole of the seaboard.
Her ambition was to extend German territory from
Cameroons across the Congo basin to join up with German
East Africa, and thus create a vast trans-continental
empire stretching from the Atlantic to the Indian Ocean.
France strenuously resisted these demands, but in the end,

by the agreement of November 1911, she sacrificed a considerable part of her equatorial possessions. The eastern border of Cameroons was greatly enlarged. But this was not all ; Germany also secured two tongues of land which gave her direct access to the Congo river and its great northern tributary the Ubangi. One of these tongues was the valley of the lower Sanga to its confluence with the Congo ; the other the valley of the Lobaye to its

"SOME" TATTOOING

confluence with the Ubangi. As they touched the rivers these strips of territory were but a few miles wide, but they sufficed Germany for the moment. Her fingers touched the coveted land, and at a later period she intended to extend her grasp. For the French, the sacrifice they had been called upon to make was painfully humiliating, for this spoliation of their territory cut the means of communication between the various colonies included in French Equatorial Africa save by river, and their colony of middle Congo was reduced to a fragment. Another territorial concession which the French felt obliged to

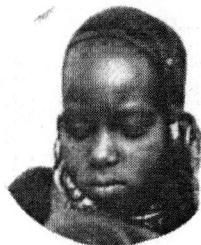

HEAD-DRESSES AND HAIR-DRESSINGS OF CAMEROON WOMEN

make revealed clearly Germany's African ambitions. When the scramble for Africa was in progress Spain had made good a claim to a squarish block of country on the coast between French Congo and Cameroons. It was known variously as Spanish Guinea or (from its chief estuary) Muni. Up to 1911 it was bounded east and south by French territory and only on the north by Cameroons. But by the 1911 agreement it became an enclave of Cameroons, the German frontier being drawn

NATIVES OF SOUTHERN PROVINCES

twenty miles south of its southern border. The Germans thus obtained the southern shores of the Muni estuary and part of Mondah Bay, and their frontier was only a few miles north of Libreville, the chief seaport of French Equatorial Africa. In area alone, the Germans by the 1911 agreement added 108,000 square miles to the Cameroons, the only return—apart from Morocco—being the cession to France of 6500 square miles in the Shari region, the German frontier there being drawn in to the Lagone river as far as its confluence with the Shari.

At the outbreak of war the total area of the German Protectorate, including the 1911 acquisitions, was about

MANENGUBA

MANDARA MOUNTAINS

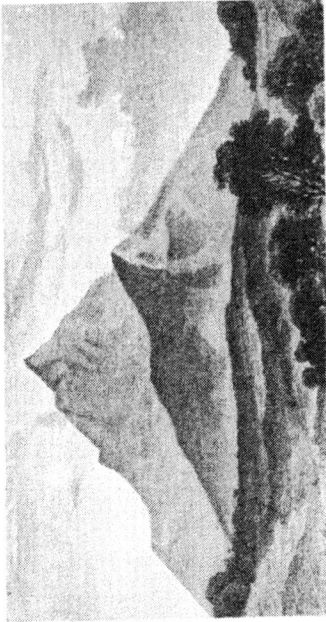

GREAT AND LITTLE CAMEROON

ATLANTIKA

E

300,000 square miles (larger than that of Germany and Great Britain combined), with an estimated population of 2000 Europears, 1700 of whom were Germans and 2,750,000 natives.

The sea frontier extended from the Rio del Ray just where the great bend of the coast line east to south begins, forming the Bight of Biafra to Mondah Bay, a distance of approximately 300 miles. The north-western boundary was conterminous with British Nigeria, running from the mouth of the Rio del Ray to the rapids of the Cross river in 8°48′ east, thence in a north-east line to within about

THE LAGONE RIVER AT MUSGAUM

30 miles of the town of Yola. It was then deflected south so as to leave Yola in British territory, turning north again to cross the Benue river at a point 3 miles west of where the Faro joins it. From here the frontier went north-east to Lake Chad, skirting its southern shore for some 40 miles. This line of demarcation was finally settled by a joint boundary commission in 1912–13. In the extreme north, British, German, and French territory met at Lake Chad. On the east and south the Colony was bordered by French Equatorial Africa. In the Bight of Biafra are the Spanish Islands of Fernando Po, Annobon, and Corisco, and those of Portugal, San Thomé, and Principe, famous for their cocoa plantations.

The Colony presents many varying types of land,

" Where Afric's swamp and mountain
Meet one on every hand."

DIE SWARTZE SCHUTZTRUPPE

GOOSE-STEPPING   AT MUSKETRY   CEREMONIAL

In a broad generalisation it may be said that the northern third is flat and open with considerable areas of swamp, save on the western border where lie the Mandara mountains. The central region is a broken plateau, mostly covered in long grass and mountainous in its western section. The third is largely covered with virgin forest almost untenanted by man, which grows thinner towards the east, finally giving place to the low and marshy valley of the Sanga. The coast region is clothed in dense vegetation and fringed with an impenetrable tangle of mangrove swamps intersected by a maze of mud creeks. There are four river systems. Those flowing into the Bight of Biafra, those feeding the Congo, those feeding the Niger, and those emptying into Lake Chad. Of the first may be mentioned the Sanaga, Njong, Campo or Ntem, and the Cameroon river or Duala, which is formed by three considerable streams, the Mungo, Wuri, and Lungasi. The first three are so greatly obstructed by bars as to be of little value as a means of communication seaward, but the Cameroon river is navigable to vessels of 20 feet draught to Duala. In the second system are the Dscha, Kadei, and Mambere, which feed the Sanga, an affluent of the Congo. In the third the Benue, the Niger's great tributary, receives the Faro and Kabea ; and in the fourth the Lagone with its numerous tributaries joins the Chari at Fort Lamy flowing into Lake Chad.

The outstanding physical feature of the Colony is its mountainous region, consisting of a huge volcanic uplift running parallel with the Nigerian frontier from the coast to within 100 miles of Lake Chad, and broken at intervals by the valleys of the Cross and Benue rivers and their tributaries. This uplift commences with the stupendous volcanic mass known as the Cameroon mountain, which rises abruptly to nearly 14,000 feet above the rocky shores and blue waters of Ambas Bay, its highest crest in winter sometimes flecked with snow. From any vantage point, but especially from the sea, it presents a magnificent spectacle, while some 30 miles westward rises Clarence Peak, 10,190 feet, the culminating point of the Island of Fernando Po. With an area on an isolated base of 700 to 800 square miles, Cameroon mountain has two distinct peaks, Great and Little Cameroon, the latter 6000 feet thickly forested to its peak. On the principal summit are a group of craters. In 1909 and again as late as 1923 the mountain was in eruption, when great streams of lava were ejected flowing through the forest to the sea. Hear what the late Mary H. Kingsley said of this wonderful mountain. " So great is its majesty and charm that every time you pass it by its beauty grows on you with greater and greater force, though it is never twice the same." Other important features in this region varying in height from 5000 to 10,000 feet are the Rumbi, the Manenguba of fantastic outline, the Atlantika, and lastly the Mandara mountains nearest to Lake Chad. On the slopes of some of these ranges

TWO OLD GENTLEMEN OF GULFEI NURSING OSTRICH " CHICKS "

primeval nature reigns supreme in the form of patches of luxuriant forest, in which are stately trees of huge dimensions with massive trunks and towering shafts rising in some cases to heights varying from 150 to 200 feet, with innumerable creepers trailing from tree to tree, a blending together of the vast and the beautiful.

The climate in general is unhealthy, the whole coastal district warm and humid, but, considering its latitude, not excessively hot, the average temperature at Duala being 78° F., with little variation throughout the year. The maximum is reached in February, the minimum in July. In the higher inland regions the climate is cooler.

Notwithstanding its comparatively moderate temperature the Cameroon coast has the reputation of being one of the most pestilential in the whole continent of Africa, while large areas are infested with the tsetse fly, in which neither horses nor cattle can live. These regions are also plagued with sleeping sickness. Malarial fever in its malignant form is frequent, and even the Africans, especially those coming from other countries, suffer from it. During the campaign it played the mischief with the allied European officers, non-commissioned officers and men, both naval and military. The rainfall is heavy in the coastal belt. From November to June is known as the " Dry," the remainder of the year the " Wet " season, but rain is liable to fall throughout the year. The average fall on the coast is about 150 inches, of which 120 falls during the " Wet " season.

The capital, Duala, consists of a group of native towns on the south bank of the Wuri river, and on the north side is the suburb of Bonaberi. Its population in 1914 was about 30,000 natives and 300 Europeans, mostly Germans. Duala was also the seat of Government, military headquarters, and the residence of merchants and missionaries. The European settlement is well planned and laid out in true German style, containing excellent buildings and tree-bordered streets, up-to-date sanitation, and a good water supply. Government House and offices are set in a picturesque park-like enclosure on a bluff overlooking the river anchorage. In the park were statues of Gustav Nachtigal and other German Colonists of note. The military cantonment, consisting of officers' mess and quarters, barracks, parade-ground, etc., is neatly planned with Prussian precision, the parade-ground worn to the level of a billiard table from years of goose-stepping by Die Swartze Schutztruppe.

The health resort and summer seat of Government is Buea, situated in the middle zone of the Cameroon mountain at about 4000 feet above sea. Having a

TWIG SUSPENSION BRIDGE

SIDE VIEW   LOOKING ACROSS   LADDER LEADING TO BRIDGE

temperate climate it affords excellent sites for sanatoria, in which jaded and fever-stricken Europeans can to some extent regain health and strength and obtain a temporary respite from the dense and enervating atmosphere of the lowlands. Victoria with its suburb Bota is a flourishing

CLOTH WEAVERS OF BAMUN

THE FINISHED ARTICLE

settlement at the base of the Cameroon mountain in Ambas Bay, while further south are the small trading ports of Kribi, Batanga, Campo, and Coco Beach. On the route from Duala to Lake Chad the most important towns are Dschang, Bamun, Joko, Banyo, and Ngaundere, the latter a large commercial centre inhabited chiefly by Hausas and first occupied by the Germans in 1901. Further north and within 30 miles of Lake Chad is Dakoa in Bornu. Kusseri on the Lagone and Gulfei on the lower Shari are also towns of some note. From Duala eastward the places of importance are Edea on the Sanaga, Yaunde, which acquired political and strategic importance during the course of the campaign, for thither after the fall of Duala the German Governor retired, making it the seat of administration and military headquarters until driven out at the close of operations. Further east towards

THE BAMENDA DRUMS

the Congo are the towns of Dume, Lomie, Cornot, Wesso, Molundu, and Bania, and south towards Spanish Muni—Ebolowa and Ambam. A number of military posts and forts had been established at various points in the Colony, but these will receive attention in later chapters.

To improve the deficient communications the Germans had planned two important lines of railway. The northern was to run the whole length of the Colony from Bonaberi to Lake Chad, but only about 100 miles of this had been completed in 1914, railhead being at Nkongsamba. The central railway which was to have run from Duala east-

wards to the Congo was in use nearly as far as Eseka,
passing through Edea on the way. On this line there
were two very fine engineering feats in the form of
steel girder bridges spanning the Lungasi at Japoma
and the Sanaga at Edea. Both were destroyed by
the Germans to impede the Allies' advance. A light
mountain railway connected Victoria and the settlements
round Ambas Bay with Soppo, the military cantonment
of Buea, and passed through many plantations on the
mountain slopes. There were plenty of roughly constructed roads throughout the Colony, but nothing of a
very permanent nature, and most of the road bridges
were of the wood trestle type. There were a number of
suspension foot-bridges made of twigs stretched over
unfordable rivers, most cleverly designed and constructed
by the natives. There was one particularly fine specimen
over the swift Dibombe river at Nlohe which had been
left intact and was of great service to us when crossing
that river in 1914.

Oversea communication with the Colony was maintained chiefly by the Woërmann line, which had a fleet
of over thirty fine vessels, passenger and cargo combined.
The German East African line steamers also called
periodically at Duala. Intercommunication by river and
creeks was kept up by small coasting vessels, launches,
and canoes. Duala was connected by submarine cable
with the British telegraph station at Bonny in the Niger
delta and with the chief towns by telegraph and telephone. The large wireless station at Duala was
destroyed by the Germans when that town surrendered
to the Allies.

The country is rich in natural products, one of the most
important being the oil palm. Cocoa cultivation was
introduced by the Germans and proved remarkably successful. Rubber is collected from the landolphia and various
species of Ficus, and there are a number of rubber plantations on the slopes of Cameroon mountain. Palm-oil,

palm-kernels, cocoa, copra, calabar beans, kola nuts, and
ivory are the principal exports, and the natives grow for
their own use bananas, yams, maize, pea-nuts, sugar-cane,
sorghum, and pepper.   There are several kinds of finely
grained woods in the forests, amongst which a very dark
ebony is specially remarkable.   Minerals have not been
found in paying quantities.   The iron is smelted by the
natives, who manufacture lances, spears, arrow-heads,
knives, swords, and hoes.   The natives are clever carvers
of wood, and make highly ornamental figure-heads for
their canoes ; they weave
cloths of beautiful colours
on their hand-looms ; they
also make wonderful drums
of hide stretched over the
open end of a hollowed-out
piece of wood ; the drum-
sticks, shaped like the figure
seven, are about an inch
in diameter. They have a
code in accordance with
which messages can be
transmitted enormous dis-

SIX FEET-TWO GORILLA

tances.   The roll of the "talking drums" echoes across
the hills from village to village, and the rapidity and
accuracy with which news travels by this means beats
even our telegraph system—no forms, no fees, no red-
tape !
    Plantations founded by German industry were fairly
successful.   Large reserves were set apart for the natives
by Government when marking off the land granted to
plantation companies.   The best known of these, the
Sud-Kamerun, held a concession over a large tract of
country by the Sanga river, exporting rubber, ivory, and
other produce via the Congo.   The principal imports
were cotton goods, spirits, building material, fire-arms,
hardware, and salt.   It is worthy of notice that, in spite

of all the German energy and enterprise, more than half the trade of the Colony was handled by three British firms, of which John Holt and Co. of Liverpool was by far the most important.

Wild animals abound in this Colony, including the great pachyderms and carnivora. The latter prey on the various kinds of antelopes which swarm on the grass lands and in the park-like areas of the central plateau. Two kinds of buffalo are found in the forests, which are also the home of the gorilla and chimpanzee. Large rodents, like the porcupine and cave rat, are numerous, and there is a diversified bird fauna, peculiar in many species.

The late Sir Harry Johnston, G.C.M.G., K.C.B., writing on the Cameroons in 1915, made the following remarks : " The British and French Governments would do well to make an exhaustive survey of this territory. Quite probably its dense forests will be found to contain beasts, birds, and reptiles new to science, as well as those interesting creatures already slightly known, such as the pigmy elephants, the ' hairy frogs,' the huge six-feet-two gorillas, the large grey chimpanzis, the black forest pigs, possibly even the okapis and other dimly known or surmised denizens of the interior forests. Even the domestic animals of the Cameroons are of special interest ; witness the pigmy sheep of the Duala and Bakundu country, unlike any other African breed, with the coloration of a mouflon and the size of a four-months'-old lamb. There are said to be huge hyenas in the north equivalent in bulk to the extinct cave variety of the spotted hyena of prehistoric Europe. There are lions in the east and north which, it is stated, retain the ancient spots on their hides, as do occasional examples in German East Africa [1]—in this last case attested by

[1] Tanganyika.

photography. There are unclassified giraffes and probably unclassified antelopes, peculiar guinea-fowl, in short, a host of marvels but little known as yet to scientific naturalists."

The human races of Cameroons are very diverse in type. The northern portion is inhabited by Fula, Hausa, and allied tribes. The Fula are numerous and powerful and spread over an immense region from Senegal to Dafur. Strictly they have no country of their own and nowhere form the whole of the population, though nearly always the dominant native race. Their most southerly Emirate

HORSEMEN OF THE ADAMUA COUNTRY

is Adamua, the country on both sides of the Upper Benue. The Hausa inhabit a very large area in the West and Central Soudan from the Niger to Bornu. Both morally and intellectually the Fula and Hausa are superior to the semi-Bantu peoples, such as the Baya, Bali, Banyang, and Bamun, who inhabit the central portion and have of late years become partly Mahomedanised. These again are superior to the Bantu coast tribes, the Duala, Bakundu, Bakwiri, Batanga, etc. The Fula and Hausa are of martial disposition, and continually waged war with their neighbours and amongst themselves until the pacification of the hinterland by Germany at the beginning of the century. The Hausas make excellent soldiers and are fine fighters.

Such is a brief description of the interesting and wonderful country which Germany, after a very stubborn resistance, was forced to surrender to the Allies.

CHAPTER IV

THE INCEPTION OF THE CAMEROON EXPEDITIONARY FORCE—THE SITUATION
IN NIGERIA—FIRST STEP TOWARDS AN OFFENSIVE—A CRUISER ORDERED
TO DUALA—ALLIED CONFERENCE OF 15TH AUGUST, 1914—MOVE-
MENTS OF H.M.S. " CUMBERLAND "—MILITARY PLANS—MODIFICATION
OF ORIGINAL PLANS—MORE GERMAN NEUTRALITY INTRIGUES—
MILITARY FORCES IN WEST AFRICA IN 1914

ON the outbreak of war columns drawn from the Nigeria Regiment were concentrated near the German frontier in accordance with a pre-arranged defence scheme, being under the orders of Colonel C. H. P. Carter, C.B., C.M.G., Commandant of the West African Frontier Force, whose headquarters were at Lagos.

There were in all five columns : two in the north based on Maidugari and Nafada in the Lake Chad region ; one based on Yola, on the Benue river, and two further south on the Cross river and near Calabar. Of these columns, that based on Yola was the strongest, consisting of four companies of infantry, one company of mounted infantry, and some mountain guns, and it faced the important German post of Garua, some twenty-five miles across the frontier.

The Governor General of Nigeria, Sir Frederick Lugard (now Lord Lugard of Abinger), was at home on leave at this time, and the Deputy Governor wired the Colonial Office on 5th August that the Commandant proposed to invade the Cameroons if circumstances were favourable, with Duala as the objective, that it was reported the French had 2000 men at Fort Lamy on the eastern frontier of the German territory, and that he was inclined to think that the Commandant was more impressed with the offensive than defensive. The reply to this wire was sent on 6th August, and stated that the general policy for the present was that no offensive action was to be taken without instructions from the Secretary of State. The Deputy Governor, in acknowledging this wire on 8th August, said that there was no offensive action. That in his previous telegram he was concerned principally with the danger of internal disturbances and attack on important posts and consequent shortage of supplies if large bodies of troops were massed on the eastern frontier, necessitating the withdrawal of the usual garrisons in the southern provinces. That he had decided on receipt of Colonial Office telegram that concentration of troops on eastern frontier was unnecessary purely for defence. That the Commandant had been instructed to confine movements of troops as far as possible to those in " precautionary stage " of defence scheme, but that Commandant was unable to consent to alterations from disposition laid down for " war stage." That in view of recent unrest in certain portions of southern provinces he requested that approval be given to modification of dispositions of troops which were originally laid down in anticipation of immediate offensive.

On 8th August the Admiralty and Colonial Office had been asked to work out details of the forces required for an expedition against Duala, and on the same evening the Deputy Governor's telegram from Nigeria asking that the disposition of the military forces in the Protectorate should be altered was received. Next day in reply inquiries were made as to whether an attack on Duala without naval co-operation was possible, and what forces could be spared from Nigeria for this purpose. A memorandum was also drawn up by the Admiralty with regard to an attack on the Cameroons. This described the objective as being the capture of Duala with its Government offices, wireless station and docks, which formed a base from which hostile naval operations could be carried out

against our trade. It was considered impossible for a
naval force to co-operate effectively with a Nigerian
expedition acting from the interior owing to the lack of

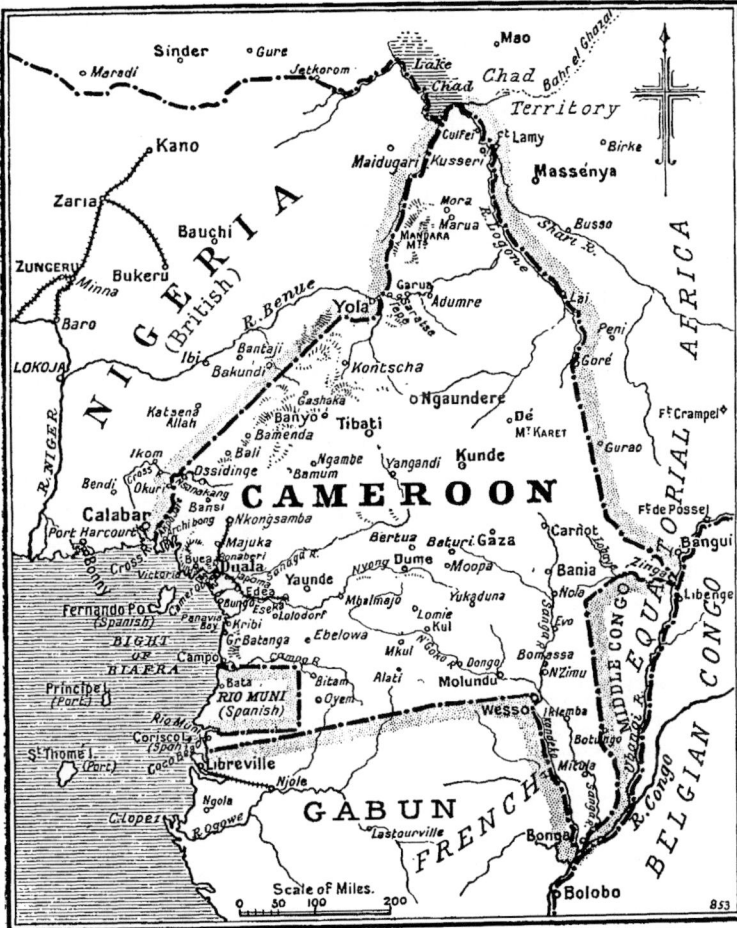

MAP OF CAMEROON.

communication and the difficult nature of the country
lying between Duala and the frontier, but it was recognised
that preliminary action along the frontier might induce
the enemy to reduce his coast garrisons and so facilitate
a direct attack on the capital and chief port. It was not

F

anticipated that the coast defences would prove formidable, and it was suggested that provided there were no German cruisers in the river the gunboat *Dwarf*, then at Sierra Leone, should convoy the transports and support the landing of the attacking force. It was, however, discovered that the *Dwarf* was under repairs and would not be ready for sea until 14th August, so that immediate action was impossible. It was then suggested that the expedition should be prepared at Sierra Leone in readiness to start at short notice, while the proposed operations on the Nigerian frontier need not be in any way affected. It was also hoped that the naval situation on the West Coast of Africa would be cleared up in the near future, for there was at this time great obscurity with regard to the movements of certain enemy war vessels. For instance, on 9th August it was reported from several sources that the Spanish wireless station at Fernando Po was in German hands and that the *Dresden*, *Eber*, and *Panther* were in those waters, and the whole uncertainty was increased by the difficulty of maintaining communication with our cruisers off the Cape Verde Islands.

It will thus be seen that on or about 10th August the naval idea was that there should be a diversion made by the Nigerian troops in the interior, while the expedition from Sierra Leone escorted by the *Dwarf* attacked Duala, the date of the latter adventure being dependent on the local naval situation. Meanwhile the Foreign Office had approached the French Government with regard to co-operating in the attack on Duala. The French in reply offered naval co-operation on the coast in any measures we might take, while, simultaneously, their troops would invade Cameroons from the Lake Chad and Middle Congo regions.

On 12th August the Colonial Office received a reply from Nigeria to the questions of 9th August to the effect that the Commandant was of opinion that naval co-operation would be required for the attack on Duala and that Nigeria could spare 2000 men and 10 guns for this service, but it was considered impracticable to co-operate with the French in the Chad or Congo regions owing to the great distances involved. Colonel Carter also advised an advance on Garua and the clearance of the north before any coast offensive was undertaken, the final form of his proposed operations being one or two columns acting from the land frontier combined with a strong attack from the sea. It was explained that in any case a preliminary reconnaissance of the frontier was essential,

H.M.S. " DWARF " LYING OFF DUALA

and on 14th August the Colonial Office approved of this being carried out provided that the forces so employed did not become involved in serious hostilities and could be easily recalled.

Meanwhile as rumour still pointed to enemy naval activity in the Bight of Biafra, the assembly of German merchantmen in the Cameroon estuary and the seizure of Fernando Po, the Admiral Commanding the Atlantic cruiser force " D " received instructions on 13th August to detach one of his ships to the Cameroons to investigate and report. Consequently the *Cumberland*, Captain Cyril Fuller (now Vice-Admiral Sir Cyril Fuller, K.C.B., C.M.G., D.S.O.), then off the Canaries, was detailed for this duty, and at a meeting of the Sub-Committee of Imperial Defence held on 14th August it was decided to postpone operations against Duala pending further information, but Brigadier General C. Dobell, C.M.G., D.S.O. (now Lieut. General Sir Charles Dobell, K.C.B., C.M.G., D.S.O.), the Inspector General of the West African Frontier Force, then in England, was called upon to prepare plans for an offensive in conjunction with the Admiralty.

It will be noticed that hitherto the expedition had been but tentatively considered, but on 15th August, as the result of an Allied conference held at the Admiralty, it assumed more definite form. The French had concentrated a force of Senegalese troops at Dakar, originally intended to reinforce their garrisons in Morocco, but our Allies later decided to use these against the Cameroons ; the joint conference was summoned to decide on the general outline of operations, and a memorandum was prepared setting forth the decisions arrived at. Fortunately just before the conference assembled a cablegram had been received from the Administrator of the Gold Coast containing information given by the native crew of the German Woërmann liner *Marina*, who had mutinied at sea and forced their officers to take the ship into a British port. Their reports showed clearly that the Germans were preparing to defend the Cameroon estuary, many ships having been sunk in the fairway, all buoys removed, and guns mounted to command the entrance. It was also reported that mines had been laid and that the gunboat *Eber* had recently left Duala. On the other hand, it appeared that there was a scarcity of native food and the population was disaffected.

In view of this information the conference recommended that a blockade of the Cameroons should be established forthwith and that the expedition should not be unduly delayed.

The French contingent from Dakar would consist of

about 2000 men and 6 field guns, while our garrison at Sierra Leone would furnish some 600 men and 6 mountain guns, and Nigeria probably about 2000 men and 10 guns. All these forces with several thousand carriers would need transporting and escort to Victoria in Ambas Bay, which at that stage was selected as the point of debarkation, the force was then to advance on Duala, said to be about six days' march distant. A number of armed launches and shallow draught gunboats were to be improvised at Lagos for creek and river work and landing troops and others

H.M.S. " CUMBERLAND "

were to be fitted out as mine-sweepers. The question as to who should command the Allied military force was left to be settled between the two Governments.

The *Cumberland*, which was proceeding to Fernando Po, coaled at Freetown on 21st August and left on the 23rd, towing the *Dwarf* and escorting the transport *Akabo*, which was bound for Lome, the port of Togoland, with a reinforcement of Sierra Leone troops for the Allied force then moving against Kamina. After dropping the *Akabo* at Lome on the 28th, the *Cumberland* and *Dwarf* made for Fernando Po via Lagos in accordance with Admiralty instructions. The French gunboat *Surprise*, having broken down, was unable to join the *Dwarf* at Sierra Leone as had been intended.

The French originally proposed that the Commander of their troops from Dakar should be in supreme command of the Allied military force of the expedition. As this, however, conflicted with the desire of the British that the Inspector General of the West African Frontier Force should be in charge of the operations, the French Government on 22nd August *de bonne grâce* agreed to place their troops under General Dobell's orders, and, with this important point settled, the final arrangements were made at home.

It is unnecessary to examine closely the details of these military plans, especially as there were subsequently constant minor modifications, but the main idea was that General Dobell with his staff would sail from England in a large vessel suitable for use as a transport, hospital ship, headquarter offices, etc. The various British Colonies and protectorates on the West Coast of Africa would meanwhile prepare their contingents for embarkation and the General would proceed down the Coast picking up troops, stores, etc., from the Gambia, Sierra Leone, Gold Coast, Togoland, and Nigeria on his way. The Colonial Office ordered the Nigerian authorities to arrange specially for the provision of a plentiful supply of surf boats suitable for landing troops on open beaches. It may here be noted that the peculiar conditions of West African warfare which render any form of animal transport in the coast zone out of the question, involve the use of a small army of native carriers—approximately three to every two fighting men. These being chiefly recruited from Sierra Leone and the Gold Coast would have to be shipped with the troops.

The formal instructions to General Dobell were drafted at a meeting of the Overseas Committee of the Committee of Imperial Defence on 27th August and were confirmed by the Government next day. They described the initial objective of the expedition as being the capture of Victoria, Buea, and Duala, particularly the wireless station at the latter place, and laid down general rules as a guide to the Commander of the force in his dealings with the French and Colonial authorities.

The Elder-Dempster liner *Appam* was taken over by the Government to convey the General and his staff to the theatre of operations and to act as a kind of floating base. She was due to leave Liverpool at the end of August and was to be escorted by the *Europa* to Sierra Leone.

YAUNDE FORT, CAMEROONS

On 29th August the Sub-Committee C.I.D. met again to consider recent and reliable information to the effect that the country between Victoria and Duala was quite impracticable for military operations during the rainy season then prevailing, and it was agreed that if this proved to be correct, the operation would have to be more of a combined naval and military character than had been contemplated ; but in view of the fact that it was hoped to make a suitable addition to the naval force, the existing arrangements were allowed to stand, any necessary modifications to be made on the spot.

It was finally decided that the *Europa* was only to escort the *Appam* to the Canaries, where she would be relieved by the cruiser *Challenger* (Captain C. P. Beaty-Pownall), which would not only act as escort but would be employed as a reinforcement in the subsequent operations. The advantage of this arrangement was that the *Challenger*, being of lighter draught than the *Cumberland*, would be able to proceed up the Cameroon estuary and attack Duala with direct fire.

The *Appam* with General Dobell and staff sailed from Liverpool on 31st August, and it was hoped the French contingent from Dakar escorted by the cruiser *Bruix* would join up at Sierra Leone.

We see from the preceding pages of this chapter that before a final decision as to the plan of action to be followed in this comparatively minor operation in the Cameroons was reached, many conferences and meetings were held at which representatives of the War Office, Admiralty, Colonial Office, Committee of Imperial Defence, and Allied Governments participated, and that following the deliberations of these councils there were orders and counter-orders, delays, local dissensions between Colonial, Civil, and Military authorities as to the application of the defence scheme, and then a series of unsuccessful actions which checked the progress of the campaign. Had the country been prepared in pre-war days with comprehensive schemes for the conquest of German African possessions, most, if not all, of the " preliminary plans " and " discussions " could have been dispensed with and the African campaigns considerably curtailed. But defence schemes were the fashion of those days in spite of the known intentions of Germany to acquire at our expense a vast African Empire.

It was at this time—towards the end of August—that the German Government made a singular *demarche*. It was just after the fight at Chra in Togoland, and the eve of the destruction of the wireless telegraphy installation at Kamina. Germany saw herself being cut off from communication with her other African Colonies, and knew already that the German Navy could not afford them any protection. She bethought herself of a declaration of the Berlin Conference of 1884–5 in favour of the neutrality of the conventional basin of the Congo and invoked it to preserve, as far as possible, her possessions in Equatorial Africa. By the Berlin Act the basin of the Congo was conventionally extended so that it included not only the Belgian Congo, but about half of French Equatorial Africa, a third of Cameroons, all German East

H.M.S. " CHALLENGER "

Africa, all British East Africa, and Uganda, all Nyassaland, the northern part of Portuguese West Africa, and a small portion of Northern Rhodesia.

In a note addressed by Herr Zimmerman, Under-Secretary of State in the German Foreign Office, to Mr. Gerard, American Ambassador in Berlin, the aid of the Unites States Government was asked to procure the neutralisation of all this region. In a subsequent communication, dated 15th September, 1914, to Mr. Gerard, Herr Zimmerman stated that Germany's object in making the proposal was " to prevent an aggravation of the state of war which could serve no purpose, while prejudicial to the community of culture of the white race." This was so far from being the truth that the Germans had made elaborate preparations to attack French Equatorial Africa ; Berlin simply sought a way of escape from a position which left it without means of succouring its Colonies. The German proposals met with no encouragement at Washington, the State Department contenting itself with forwarding—without any observations—the German proposal to the Governments concerned, and the Governments concerned refused to entertain Berlin's overtures.

German diplomacy tried hard to prove that it was the Allied Powers which " violated the neutrality " of the Congo basin. As to that, the text of the Berlin Act left the declaration of neutrality in the Congo basin optional, not obligatory, and the only State affected by the Berlin Act whose African territory had been declared neutral was Belgium. At its foundation the Congo Free State proclaimed its perpetual neutrality, and when that State became a Belgian Colony the obligation of neutrality was taken over. And Belgium had loyally endeavoured to preserve neutrality on the Congo, even after the violation by Germany of Belgium's own neutrality. Belgium, for some time, endeavoured to preserve the Belgian Congo neutral, and it was not until 28th August, 1914, when the movements of German columns towards the Ubangi and the Middle Congo constituted a direct menace to Belgian territory—which, moreover, had been attacked by Germans in the Tanganyika region—that the Governor General of the Congo, M. Fuchs, was granted permission to assist the French in the campaign in the Cameroons. This help M. Merlin, the Governor General of French Equatorial Africa, asked for, and on 30th September Belgian forces were placed at his disposal. The German allegation that the Belgians began hostilities by seizing the port of Zinga on the Ubangi on 7th August was false ; the first act of war in Belgian Congo was committed by the Germans when their steamer *Hedwig von Wissmann*,

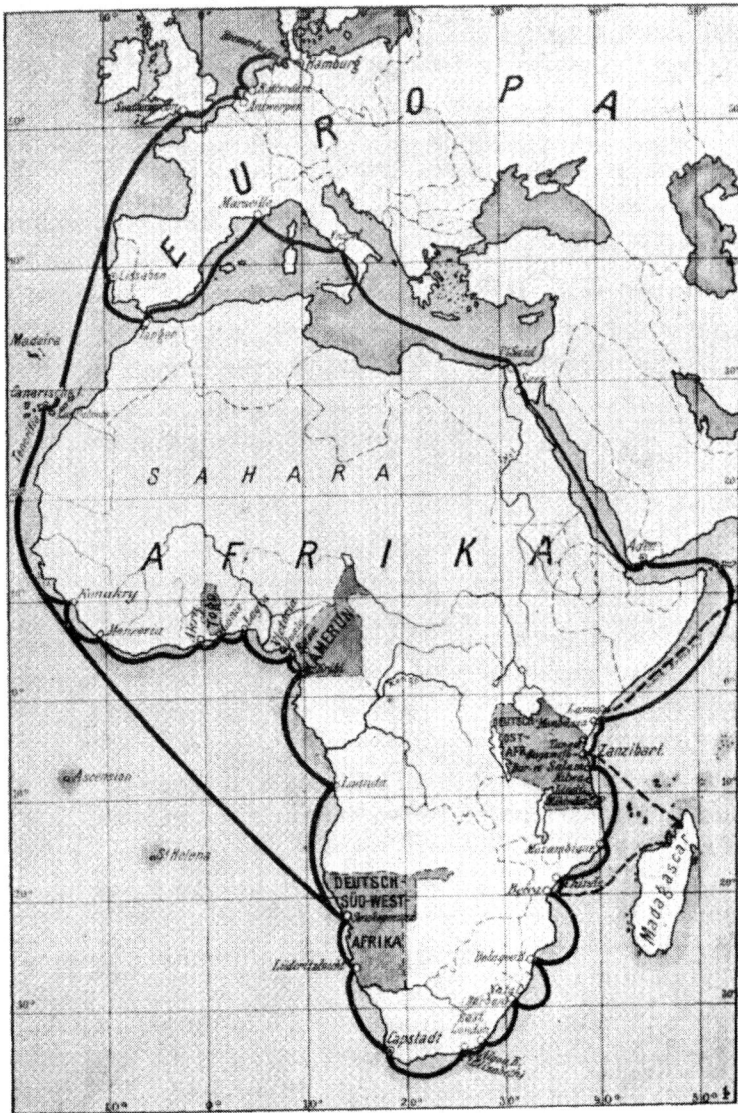

MAP SHOWING GERMANY'S PRE-WAR AFRICAN COLONIES AND PORTS
SERVED BY HER SHIPPING

on 22nd August, bombarded the Belgian port of Lukaga (Albertville) on Lake Tanganyika.

In August 1914 the British troops on the West Coast of Africa, from which an Expeditionary Force could be drawn, consisted of :—

(1) The Imperial Garrison of the Sierra Leone Colony under the War Office, the detail of which is given in Chapter II. (2) The West African Frontier Force or " Waffs " administered by the Colonial Office and distributed as follows :—

Gambia	The Gambia Company.
Sierra Leone	The Sierra Leone Battalion.
Gold Coast	The Gold Coast Regiment.
	1 Battery Mountain Artillery.
	1 Battalion Infantry.
Nigeria	2 Batteries Mountain Artillery.
	4 Battalions Infantry.
	1 Battalion Mounted Infantry.

The approximate strength of these forces was :— 350 British officers and N.C.O.'s, 150 British Fortress Artillery and Royal Engineers, and 8000 native troops with thirty 2·95 M.M. Hotchkiss Q.F. mountain guns. The headquarters of the " Waffs " consisted of an Inspector General with the temporary rank of Brigadier General and two staff officers. The Inspector General was military adviser to the Colonial Office on all matters concerning the force, and he periodically inspected its various units. In certain instances he took command in the field. His headquarters were at the Colonial Office.

In addition to these regular forces, in each Colony and Protectorate there were a number of Europeans employed by trading firms, shipping companies, mines, banks, and business houses. Some of these enrolled as volunteers with the Expeditionary Force and performed yeoman service. There were also police, administrative, medical, and marine officers of the Colonial Civil Service, many of whom served with distinction throughout the war. The French could furnish contingents from their vast West African possessions of Senegal, Guinea, Dahomey, Chad and Ubangi regions and French Congo (Gabon). The regular military forces in the four French territories bordering the Cameroons consisted at the outbreak of war of the following units under the orders of General Aymerich, the Commander-in-Chief of French Equatorial

MOUNTAIN GUN, NIGERIAN ARTILLERY, IN ACTION

Africa, whose headquarters were at Brazzaville, Middle Congo :—

(1) *In Chad* was the 4th (Chad) Regiment comprising ten companies of infantry, a squadron of cavalry, mountain artillery section, a section of machine-guns, and a small camel corps of two companies. *Strength,* 220 French, 2300 native ranks.

(2) *In Ubangi-Shari,* the 3/3 Senegalese Tirailleurs of six companies. *Strength,* 90 French, 1160 natives.

(3) *In Middle Congo,* the 2/2 Senegalese Tirailleurs of six companies. *Strength,* 115 French, 1190 natives.

(4) The Gabon Regiment. *Strength,* 150 French, 1370 natives. But with a frontier to guard of 2000 miles, not

a large number of troops could be drawn from these forces for offensive action at the opening stages of hostilities.

The Belgians also could supply a few troops from the Congo.

Of these forces, at the commencement of operations the British and French could put into the field for overseas operations about 3000 men each. The enemy strength could only be estimated. According to official statistics, the regular military force in the Cameroons consisted of about 200 German officers and N.C.O.'s and 2000 native troops supplemented by an armed police force of some 60 Germans and 1500 natives. In reality, however, the force actually employed in the opening stages of the campaign seems to have approximated 800 Europeans and at the lowest estimate 6000 natives, the European number being reached by calling up all Germans in the Colony, including the crews of the fleet of merchantmen which on the eve of war sought refuge in the Cameroon estuary. The bulk of their force was well trained, armed, and led, and plentifully supplied with machine-guns, deadly weapons if skilfully handled in the Forest and Bush. The Germans also had a number of fortified posts in the Colony, all placed with an eye to military requirements. Colonel Zimmerman, the Commander of the troops, faced with tremendous odds, proved himself an able and resourceful soldier.

As the " Waffs " took so important a share, not only in the conquest of the Cameroons, but of East Africa and Togoland also, a few remarks concerning the units of which it is composed might here be appropriately recorded. The strongest unit, the Nigeria Regiment, grew out of the old Royal Niger Company Constabulary and the forces of the old Lagos Colony and Niger Coast Protectorate. In view of the critical situation that followed French encroachments on the territory of the Niger Company from 1894–7, the British Government decided to raise a local force, and

Colonel Lugard was sent out to organise and command it. By 1900 the force had become a thoroughly well-organised and disciplined corps, which Lugard named the West African Frontier Force. At the end of 1901 all the Colonial military forces in British West Africa were modelled on the same basis and under the same designation. The Northern Nigeria Regiment consisted of two Batteries of Mountain Artillery and two Battalions of Infantry, to which was added later a third Mounted Infantry Battalion. At the same time the Lagos Battalion and the Niger Coast Protectorate Force, with a portion of the Royal Niger Company Constabulary, became the Southern Nigeria Regiment of the " Waffs." On the amalgamation of Lagos and Southern Nigeria, the Lagos Battalion became the 2nd Battalion of the Southern Nigerian Regiment. When Northern and Southern Nigeria were amalgamated on 1st

TWO W.A.F.F. OFFICERS

January, 1914, the two regiments became one, which was designated the Nigeria Regiment, consisting of two Batteries of Mountain Artillery, four Battalions of Infantry, and one Battalion of Mounted Infantry.

The regiment has a fine record of service in peace and war. In 1922 it received its first colours, which bear the following battle honours: " Ashantie 1873–4," " Ashanti 1900," " Behobeho," " Nyango," " East Africa 1916–18," " Duala," " Garua," " Banyo," " Cameroons 1914–16."

From September 1914 to the end of the War the regiment was commanded by a distinguished and most active soldier, Brigadier General Cunliffe, C.B., C.M.G., Commander Legion of Honour.

Then came the Gold Coast Regiment. From 1843 to 1852 a small Imperial garrison in the shape of a company of the West India Regiment was maintained in the Gold Coast, but in the latter year it was decided to raise a local force in the Colony to be called the Gold Coast Corps, and the West India Company was withdrawn. The corps was 300 strong, and was trained as an artillery unit and recruited mainly from redeemed slaves of the tribes inhabiting the country now known as the Northern Territories. In 1857 this corps was renamed the Gold Coast Artillery Corps. It was not very reliable, however, and was disbanded in 1863, when garrison duties were once more taken over by the West India Regiment. In 1873 the Gold Coast Rifle Corps of Volunteers was formed for service with Wolseley's force against the Ashantis. In 1865 a local corps of Hausas had been raised for service in Lagos, then a dependency of the Gold Coast, which in 1873 also took part in Wolseley's campaign under Captain Glover, R.N., and at the end of the War 350 of its members remained in the Gold Coast and formed the nucleus of the Gold Coast Constabulary, which was raised in 1879, its establishment being 16 British officers and 1203 native ranks. It fought in the campaigns of Tengi 1885, Jebu 1892, Ashanti 1895–6, Northern Territories 1897–8, Atabobo and Ashanti 1900.

In 1901, on the amalgamation of the Colonial military forces in West Africa into the " Waffs," the Gold Coast Constabulary became the Gold Coast Regiment organised into two battalions. The 1st, composed of a Battery of mountain guns and nine companies of Infantry, had its headquarters at Kumasi, with detachments at Accra and other important ports in the colony. The 2nd Battalion, consisting of a Battery and six companies, was stationed

THE " WAFFS " IN THE TRENCHES

G

in the Northern Territories with headquarters at Gambaga, but on 1st July, 1907, this battalion was disbanded, some of its officers and men joining the new Northern Territories Constabulary. In 1914 the regiment consisted of a Battery of Mountain Artillery and nine companies of Infantry, and was commanded by Lieut. Col. R. A. De B. Rose, the Worcester Regiment.

In the Great War the Gold Coast Regiment took a prominent part in the conquest of Togoland 1914, Cameroons 1914–16, and East Africa 1916–18, gaining for itself a great reputation, and rendered such valuable services in these campaigns that the War Office asked for the formation of a Gold Coast Brigade for service in Palestine, but the Armistice with Turkey was concluded before its organisation could be completed.

The third unit of the " Waffs "—the Sierra Leone Battalion—may be said to have commenced its history with the raising of the Sierra Leone Police in August 1829. Its strength was then 17 officers and 325 men, recruited from liberated slaves of Freetown. In the year 1890, after varying fortunes and honourable services in the hinterland, it became the Sierra Leone Frontier Police, and in 1901 the Sierra Leone Battalion of the West African Frontier Force.

Its services include the Tambi Expedition 1892, Suppression of Sofa raids 1893–4, Gambia Expedition 1894, the quelling of the Sierra Leone rebellion 1898–9, Ashanti War 1900–1. Whilst in the Great War it served in Togoland and Cameroons 1914–16, where it fought some hard fights and suffered many casualties, including its gallant Commanding Officer, Lieut. Col. G. P. Newstead.

For all these services His Majesty the King was graciously pleased to award colours to the regiment, which were presented by His Excellency Sir A. R. Slater, K.C.M.G., Governor and Commander-in-Chief of Sierra Leone, at Daru on 27th May, 1922.

There is a regimental custom in this unit which has

been strictly observed since the year 1892, when a Major Moore of the Royal Irish Fusiliers taught the native soldiers to sing a verse of the National Anthem every night after tattoo roll-call. Shortly afterwards, a native officer of the Battalion, not to be outdone, taught his men to say the Lord's Prayer. And now at 8.30 p.m. daily at headquarters, on detachment or the line of march the men sing " God save the King," and then say the Lord's Prayer. At Regimental Headquarters, after the prayer, the Benediction is given by the Band Sergeant, after which the parade is dismissed.

THE NATIVE TOWN, DUALA, CAPITAL OF THE CAMEROONS

The fourth unit of the " Waffs " is the Gambia Company, which was raised in 1901 to replace the Imperial garrison of one company of the West India Regiment for service in the Gambia.

In the *London Gazette* of 23rd June, 1925, it was announced that His Majesty the King had been graciously pleased to accept the position of Colonel-in-Chief of the West African Frontier Force, an honour greatly appreciated by all ranks of this distinguished corps.

Whilst on the subject of armed forces, a brief reference to the general attitude of the native populations of our West African territories from which the soldiers who fought our battles were recruited may not be out of place. Their attitude from the commencement of the War, in so far as their minds could grasp the nature of the great upheaval, was one of loyalty and sympathy for the British. A few minor incidents occurred for which the absence of troops and scarcity of political and administrative officers were mainly responsible, but the important chiefs throughout the countries gave tangible proof of their loyalty. Considerable sums of money were provided towards defraying the expenses of the campaigns, and the inhabitants, in spite of the greatly increased cost of living, subscribed freely to the Red Cross, the Prince of Wales' and other War funds.

CHAPTER V

THE *Cumberland* and the *Dwarf* duly arrived at Lagos on 29th August, when Captain Fuller was notified by telegram from the Admiralty that the *Appam* was about to sail from Liverpool with General Dobell, with whom he should co-operate on his arrival. In the meanwhile Fuller was to gain as much intelligence as possible and to make preparations for a direct attack on Duala by light draught vessels.

A conference was held at Lagos between the naval Commanding Officers and the Colonial authorities, as a result of which Captain Fuller was given complete control of the flotilla of small vessels which composed the Nigerian Marine, and the Government workshops at Apapa were placed at his disposal.

Here we come in contact for the first time with the Nigerian Marine. Beyond the limits of the coast region little was known in pre-war days of this department and its important and useful rôle. The credit for opening up and keeping open the numerous waterways of the Niger delta and other rivers, amounting to hundreds of miles of mangrove-bordered mud creeks, was due to its officers who were continuously engaged in supervising this dangerous, difficult, and unhealthy work. Many of them laid down their lives during the course of the campaign.

The officers were, as a rule, selected from the Mercantile Marine and had nearly all served in the Royal Naval Reserve. The material used in this creek work was just the kind likely to be useful in the Cameroon estuary, consisting as it did of all kinds of small craft, from the branch boat (used for carrying mails and passengers from Lagos to outlying towns on the coast and up the rivers) to the small motor-boat, including also powerful tugs and roomy motor-launches. In addition there was a well-equipped dockyard at Apapa (in the lagoon opposite Lagos) capable of building and repairing small craft and keeping the existing flotilla efficient. All the labour was native, supervised by the white officers, and the whole department was controlled by a director, responsible to the Governor. The late Lieutenant H. A. Childs, C.M.G., a retired officer of the Royal Navy, was director in 1914, and he and his officers to a man volunteered to accompany the expedition. The detailed arrangements made will be described later, but the work of fitting small craft for mine-sweeping was commenced at once.

It was at Lagos that " King Bell," brother of the native chief hanged by the Germans at Duala for having sought the help of the English, was embarked with other natives with a knowledge of the Cameroons country, who were to act as pilots, guides, spies, etc. "Guns Q.F.C.", in his interesting *Account of a Cruiser's Operations in the Cameroons*, remarks : " The heat at this time was very oppressive, temperatures in the stokehold frequently rising to 130° F., and natives (*Kroomen*) were therefore engaged to trim coal in the ship's bunkers, to man the surf boats when landing over bars, and for other useful work. These natives had to be borne on the ship's books for pay purposes. Some had no names and others were blessed with patronymics which so baffled the accountant staff that they were made to select " tallies " for entry in the ship's ledger. Undoubtedly they were assisted by the sailors in their choice, which accounts for the appearance in the books of such distinguished personages as Lloyd George, Kitchener, Try Best, Snowball, Sea-breeze, etc. To see Lloyd George receive seven shillings as a reward for a week's labours was the source of undisguised mirth of both officers and men." Having settled these matters the *Cumberland* left Lagos in the evening (29th August) and proceeded to Fernando Po, arriving off that island on the morning of 31st August. The anchorages in Carlos and Isobel Bays were examined, but no signs of enemy activity were discovered, so that the reports received by the Admiralty as to the presence of German cruisers in those waters proved to be unfounded. " Had they been there," as " Guns Q.F.C." aptly puts it, " it is extremely improbable that the *Cumberland* would have taken any subsequent interest in this or any other campaign." It was in fact discovered that the last German warship sighted was the *Eber* and that she had left as long ago as May. After interviewing the Spanish Governor of the island, who satisfied Captain Fuller that he had maintained strict neutrality, the *Cumberland* proceeded towards the Cameroons coast, but we must not leave Fernando Po

FEATHERED CHIEF OF THE CAMEROONS

behind us without mentioning that it is the largest and perhaps also the most beautiful of all the isles off this coast, a great volcanic mass with many forest-crowned craters culminating in Clarence Peak, called by the Spaniards " Pico de Santa Isabel " and by the natives

" O Wassa." Viewed from the slopes of its great brother, Cameroon mountain, twenty miles across the Straits, it looks like an immense single cone floating out to sea and against the sunset like a fairy isle of gold. Other fragments from this island are that the " Fanny Po " ladies are celebrated for their beauty up and down the coast, and that among the domesticated animals are the Clarence pigs, a breed imported by the Spaniards. The late Mary Kingsley in her interesting book on West Africa tells us that these animals at one time became such a nuisance

BAMENDA HORSEMEN

BAMUN CAVALRYMAN AND
" CHINDA " OR KING'S MESSENGER

and so destructive to gardens and crops that the Governor issued instructions that all pigs seen without rings in their noses would be destroyed, and the proclamation was conveyed to the inhabitants by the native town crier thus : " I say—I say—I say—I say—Suppose pig walk—Iron no live for him nose !—gun shoot—Pop—Kill 'im one time—Hear re— Hear re ! " But we must leave the pigs and return to our sheep. The Cumberland arrived at the mouth of the Cameroon estuary on the evening of 31st August, where she drove in a merchantman which was patrolling off the entrance ; owing, however, to the possibility of the bar being mined a closer examination could not then be carried out, and as the German wireless station at Duala was completely jamming communication with Lagos, Captain Fuller decided to make for Calabar river, the nearest Nigerian port, to communicate the result of his cruise by cable to the Admiralty. He arrived off Calabar on 1st September.

During his visit to Lagos on 29th August, Fuller had arranged for five of the Nigerian Marine vessels to be fitted for mine-sweeping, and the necessary gear was prepared in the Government dockyard with great expedition. The vessels fitted were the *Ivy*, Government yacht, armed with a 12 pdr. and two 3 pdr. guns ; *Balbus* and *Walrus*, steam-tugs ; *Alligator* and *Crocodile*, large motor-launches, each 100 feet long. In addition two 80-feet steam-launches, *Vampire* and *Vigilant*, were each armed with a 3 pdr. and maxims for service with the expedition, while two large tugs, *Remus* (screw) and *Porpoise* (paddle), were fitted with steel protection to the bridge preparatory to being armed with 12 pdrs. from the *Cumberland*. All these vessels were manned and com-

FLEET OF CANOES ON CAMEROON RIVER

manded by the Nigerian Marine and performed much useful service during the amphibious warfare among the swamps and creeks and up the rivers, carrying and supporting the troops.

Before describing the movements and work of the Navy which prepared the way for the landing of the troops at Duala, it will be as well to give a general outline of the local topography.

The seaward limit of the so-called Cameroon river is defined by Cape Cameroon on the north and the long narrow strip of land ending at Suellaba Point on the south. These capes are five miles apart, but the navigable channel is reduced by shoals off Suellaba Point, while about seven miles to seaward is a bar with only four fathoms at low water. The average rise of tide is six feet, with little difference between springs and neaps. The expanse of water within the points is in reality more an extensive estuary or basin than a river being formed by the junction of a number of streams. The main axis of this estuary runs north-east, coinciding with the direction of the Duala river until it divides into the Abo and Wuri branches, thirty miles from the sea. The low-lying land surrounding the estuary is intersected with small streams, which wind deviously among mangrove swamps, each stream silently rolling down its mass of sand-laden waters and constituting each in itself a pretty problem to the navigator by its network of intercommunicating creeks. The estuary itself consists of a central pool with depths from five to thirteen fathoms, gradually shoaling towards the Duala river and three large bays, all much obstructed by evil-smelling mud-flats on which crocodiles disport themselves. Monaka Bay is on the eastern side and forms the approach to the Lungasi river, accessible only by small craft. This river runs in a generally north-easterly direction, and at Yapoma, twelve miles from the entrance, is spanned by a steel girder bridge—one of the finest in Africa, over half a mile in length—which carries the Midland Railway. Two narrow creeks called Doctor and Olga connect the Lungasi with the Duala river a few miles below the town, whilst the Kwa Kwa in the south connects with the Sanaga river. Navigation in the main stream is much impeded by sand-banks ; there is, however, a channel up to the town with a least depth of 15 feet at low water. Duala itself is sixteen miles from Suellaba Point, and the river is about a mile wide abreast of the town. Bonaberi on the opposite shore is a short distance above Mungo Creek which connects with the Mungo river. On the western side of the estuary are Modeaka and Mokushu Bays, the former being the most northerly and providing an outlet for the Mungo river ; both bays are connected by a maze of small creeks with the Bimbia river, which enters the sea twelve miles west of Cape Cameroon, and may be considered as the western boundary of the waterlogged region. The depth of the creeks varies greatly with the seasons. In the rains most of them are navigable to small steamers, but in the dry will only take canoes and shallow launches. In common with those on the eastern side of the estuary they form a valuable and secret means of communication and were extensively used by the Germans.

KEKA HAVEN IN THE MANGROVES WHERE BRITISH FORCE LANDED FOR MARCH ON BUEA

The Bimbia river itself is a considerable stream as far as Tiko, ten miles inland, but is blocked from the sea by a two-fathom bar. To the westward of the Bimbia river the character of the country completely changes as the spurs of the great mountain come down to the coast, which is steep, wooded, and fringed with rocky isles and pinnacled rocks. These " summer isles of Eden " are veritable gems of beauty, but give them a wide berth, for they are also fever-traps of the worst description. There are numerous settlements along this coast, the most important being

Victoria, inside Ambas Bay, which has already been mentioned. It is important to note the diverse character of the surroundings of Victoria and Duala, the two towns being but thirty miles apart as the crow flies.

The original plan of operations had been to avoid a direct attack on the defences of Duala by landing in Ambas Bay and marching a force overland through Buea, which operation, it was estimated, would take about a week. But later intelligence had shown that owing to the impassable state of the country in the wet season this plan would probably be impracticable, and on 2nd September the Admiralty informed Captain Fuller that a direct attack on Duala would, after all, be necessary. He was ordered to prepare to arm launches, which, in fact, he had already done. This message was sent to Fuller at Calabar, but the *Cumberland* had sailed for Fernando Po, and the information was not received until 10th September ; her Captain, however, had already decided that the occupation of Victoria was desirable for naval reasons. The end of the rainy season in this region, like the commencement, is accompanied by off-shore squalls of short duration but extreme violence and dangerous, especially to small craft such as composed the Nigerian flotilla, and as the defences at the entrance to the Cameroon estuary were of unknown strength it was considered essential to establish a preliminary base in Ambas Bay, where the flotilla could shelter in safety. A request was therefore made that Victoria, which was then believed to have been evacuated by the enemy, should be occupied by our troops, but on 4th September this request was negatived by the Colonial Office pending the arrival of General Dobell and the Expeditionary Force.

Meanwhile on 3rd September the *Cumberland* coaled at sea and was joined by the *Dwarf*. The empty collier was sent back to Calabar with telegrams notifying Fuller's intention of sweeping Ambas Bay on the 4th with a view to sheltering the flotilla shortly expected to join him from

Lagos. The sweeping was duly carried out by the picket-boats, and the islets in the bay were examined without discovering anything suspicious. As the bay was found to be clear of mines the *Dwarf* was sent in to deliver an ultimatum to the Governor, stating that if any opposition was made to a landing the town would be bombarded. The answer to this was that, as there was no one to resist the landing, assent must be given. Consequently a party of seventy-five seamen and marines which had been

VICTORIA IN AMBAS BAY

standing by was at once disembarked with orders to reconnoitre the town and surrounding country, to gain as much intelligence as possible, and to make preparations for the removal of any large quantities of food which might be found in Victoria or Bota. It is interesting to note here that, by means of wireless telegrams, the Germans in the Cameroons had been continually informed of colossal German victories both on land and sea, and only a short time before the arrival of the British ships " the greater part of the Grand Fleet was sent to the bottom," one paper going so far as to give a graphic account of Admiral Jellicoe's death on the quarter-deck of the flagship in true Nelson style.

The Governor therefore naturally expected help at any moment from German cruisers, which, he knew, must be available if the reports were true, and doubtless he hoped these would arrive whilst the landing-party was ashore.

It was discovered that nearly all stores of food had been removed from Victoria inland after the first appearance of our ships, and that though there were no troops actually in the vicinity the heights commanding the roads and railway leading out of the town were strongly entrenched. After destroying the local telephone exchange the force was withdrawn, but as a large stock of food was later reported by the *Dwarf* at Bota, about two miles to the westward, the men were landed again at 9 p.m. and remained ashore all night with the intention of removing the stores to the ships in the morning. This work had hardly commenced at daybreak when it was discovered that the bush surrounding the settlements was full of German troops, evidently brought up from Duala through the creeks and from Soppo, the military station of Buea, by rail, and at about 8 a.m. on 5th September the German Commander demanded immediate evacuation. It must be realised that our landing-party was to all intents and purposes a fatigue-party employed in collecting and moving the food, and that only a few men could be spared as a covering force over a fairly wide perimeter. Those on board the ships were ignorant of the course events had taken ashore until the receipt of a signal message giving a précis of the German ultimatum, which was duly reported to the Captain of the *Cumberland* at the moment when he had just hooked a ten-pound fish, being engaged in catch-his breakfast from the quarter-deck ; the ten-pounder returned to the Atlantic followed by the rod, and orders were at once given for the landing-party to return to their ships. According to statements made by the men, part of the night ashore had been spent in destroying a store containing liquor, the wantonness of which so touched their sensitive natures that any subsequent reference to the incident was invariably embellished with picturesque phraseology of the sea. As soon as the men were aboard, and after giving due warning, the *Cumberland* quickly demolished by shell-fire all the store sheds at Bota, including those containing the entire cocoa crop of the Colony.

These minor measures on the part of the Navy went to show that Victoria was untenable as a shore base owing to the densely bushed heights by which it was surrounded, while the bay itself was too open to the heavy Atlantic swell for ships to ride comfortably at anchor. The fact that troops from Duala had been brought up in a few hours by launches through the creeks, whereas we had estimated it to be a six-day overland march, proved the importance to us of the water communications necessitating control not only over the estuary, but the creeks and bays surrounding it prior to the arrival of the Expeditionary Force.

A NATIVE CHIEF, CAMEROON HINTERLAND

After dark on 5th September the *Cumberland* and *Dwarf* left the bay for a rendezvous five miles to the south of Ambas Island, where they met the first contingent of the Nigerian Flotilla under Commander R. H. W. Hughes, R.N.R. (now Captain Hughes, C.B., C.S.I., C.M.G., D.S.O., etc.), consisting of the *Ivy*, *Walrus*, and *Vampire*,

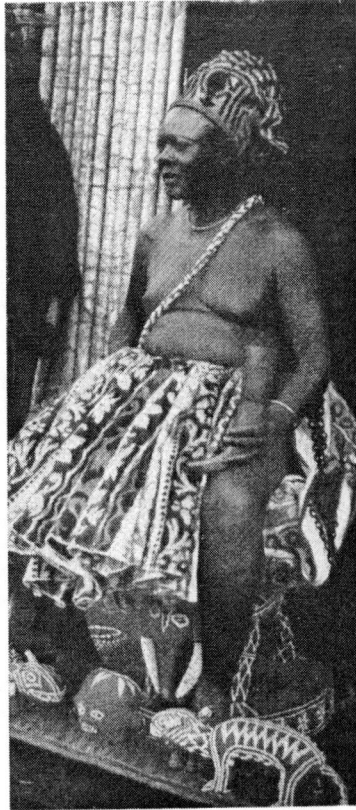

with the steam lifeboat *Moseley*. The *Walrus* had in tow a lighter filled with explosives, improvised mines, and other useful material from Lagos. As there had been a rumour in Victoria that German gunboats were in Bimbia river the *Dwarf* was told off to reconnoitre across the bar, which she did on 6th September without finding any game. Captain Fuller then planned a small night operation ; before leaving Ambas Bay he had observed several

FORT LOLODORF, 80 MILES S.W. OF YAUNDE, CAMEROONS

useful lighters alongside Victoria pier, and these he decided to capture during the night of 6th–7th September. As this little exploit savours of the old cutting-out days, it is here given as described by " Guns Q.F.C." Twenty picked men were armed with revolvers, and as the success of the operation was likely to be marred by discovery they were provided with india-rubber soled shoes to enable them to move noiselessly on the decks of the lighters, white caps were discarded and no equipment was worn.

SUNKEN SHIPS BLOCKING THE CHANNEL TO DUALA

H

The party embarked on the *Walrus* and *Vampire*, and under the guidance of the *Dwarf* with all lights extinguished they approached and boarded the lighters, apparently unobserved ; mooring chains were slipped, ropes made fast, and the whole lot taken in tow in a very short space of time in complete silence. All were successfully removed and brought to the rendezvous without a shot being fired. The *Vampire* struck a rock on the return journey and was badly damaged, but there were no casualties. We learnt later from the German Commandant of troops in Victoria that he had seen our men come in, but thinking we were landing them for a surprise attack, he had given orders to his men not to fire until ours had left the boats. In the darkness, however, he had mistaken the lighters for our boats filled with troops, and when he saw the flotilla leaving the pier with something in tow he believed we had changed our mind about landing. He confessed his surprise and chagrin when at daylight he discovered that " *All zee lighters 'ad gone.*" The shallows (extending in some places to great distances), the flat coast-line, morning mists, and the almost total absence of well-defined features make the approach to the coast in these regions a matter of anxiety to the navigator, and when, added to these difficulties, all aids such as channel and danger-marking buoys are removed, his lot is hard indeed. On 7th September ships of war shepherding the flotilla proceeded to the charted position of the Cameroon Fairway buoy off Suellaba Point to find that, in common with all other navigational marks, it had vanished : it was fortunate, therefore, that even in the prevailing bad weather a fairly secure anchorage was found, but before any further move could be made it was essential that extensive mine-sweeping should be carried out, that the channel should be surveyed and fresh buoys laid to mark the Hunds Kopje (Dog's Head) and other shoals before the *Cumberland* could venture across the bar.

On 8th September the sweeping was carried out by

the *Balbus*, *Walrus*, and *Crocodile*, directed by Lieut. Commander R. Sneyd (now Captain and D.S.O.), the *Cumberland's* torpedo officer, and though much hampered in the work by the heavy swell and strong tides a sufficient area was cleared to enable the *Cumberland* to cross the bar and anchor within six miles of Suellaba Point before dark. The following day, whilst the sweepers continued their work through the channel, parties of marines were landed at both headlands commanding the entrance to investigate

ARMED GUARD OF NATIVE CHIEF, NORTHERN CAMEROONS

—just to see if there was anything or anybody likely to be of interest to the Navy ! Cape Cameroon was found to be a mere swamp, through which the men floundered, and it was obvious no defences could be erected there, but on Suellaba Point a signal station was seized and the party of Germans manning it taken prisoners. These men were pleased that their labours were ended, for existence under the climatic conditions prevailing in that pestilential spot must have been a misery, there being no cover from the dismal downpour.

The sweepers having now cleared the outer bar, the

Dwarf was sent into the estuary to reconnoitre. After rounding Suellaba she sighted in Manoka Bay, aground and apparently abandoned, the Hamburg-Amerika steamer *Kamerun*, 3700 tons, which had been stationed off the entrance as a look-out. Her first orders had been to sink herself in the fairway should a large enemy vessel appear, and to ram a small one, a task her crew appear to have regarded with little enthusiasm, and her Captain had on 8th September run her aground undamaged, her crew escaping in the boats through the Kwa Kwa creek to Edea. The *Dwarf* then followed the sweepers up the estuary and sighted an obstruction of several sunken ships and lighters off Rugged Point. Patrolling near them was the German Government yacht *Hertzogin Elizabeth* on which the *Dwarf* opened fire, causing her to withdraw at full speed. It was noticed that she rounded the southern end of the obstruction, indicating a clear channel for light draught vessels. As sweeping operations were still progressing the *Dwarf* was unable to pursue and so withdrew. Early next morning (10th September) the *Cumberland* entered the estuary, anchoring north-east of Suellaba Point, thus completing the first step towards the establishment of a secure base.

This position was used as the main base until the fall of Duala. Its advantages were that the anchorage was good from all points of view, with sufficient depth and room for a large number of warships, transports, colliers, etc., to ride in safety. Though some distance from Duala, it commanded a view of the entire river entrance and the mouths of the numerous creeks and was sufficiently far from the latter to be immune from surprise attacks. The entrance to the outer channel was within range of the *Cumberland's* guns, and our ships could not be seen by vessels intending to enter the estuary, an important point, as the position of certain German cruisers had not been definitely established at this time. The initial disadvantage was the lack of means of communication, but steps were at once taken to remedy this defect. As all attempts at wireless were frustrated by the enemy station at Duala jamming our signals a despatch boat was sent to Calabar (100 miles), and in this way the cable ship *Transmitter* was brought down from Freetown. After carrying out repairs to the submarine cable *en route* she brought the end of it to her instruments and within two days of her arrival took up her station as cable ship at the main base. From this time onwards Duala was in uninterrupted and direct communication with London.

CHAPTER VI

GERMAN PREPARATIONS AT DUALA—NATIVE DISAFFECTION—TERRORISM —NAVAL ACTIVITY 10TH TO 12TH SEPTEMBER—THE "NACHTIGAL" EPISODE—TORPEDO ATTACK ON THE "DWARF"—SINKING OF THE "NACHTIGAL"—FURTHER BOAT RECONNAISSANCES—CLEARANCE AND BUOYAGE OF THE MAIN CHANNEL—MILITARY OPERATIONS ON THE NIGERIAN FRONTIER

THE Germans in Duala seem to have been by no means so well prepared to defend their capital as might have been anticipated. In 1913 the cruiser *Bremen* visited the port, and her Captain drew up a report emphasising its value and proposing that an elaborate defence scheme should be adopted ; nothing, however, had been done to carry out these suggestions.

After the outbreak of war a battery of guns was placed on Yoss Point, commanding the fairway to Duala, which was further defended by an obstruction of sunken ships off Rugged Point. Altogether nine had been scuttled to block the channel, gaps being filled in by lighters loaded with concrete. Two or three ships, if properly placed, would have effectively barred the passage for deep-draught vessels ; but the sinking operations were obviously conducted by an amateur with more material than knowledge, who placed six vessels on the shoals clear of the channel ! The ebb stream during the rains runs very swiftly at this point, a speed of five knots being quite common, a fact which to some extent may have contributed to the waste of material. After the arrival of our forces at the base the enemy hastily improvised a large number of mines from local resources, which, however, did not prove very formidable weapons, the only casualties caused by them being four Germans blown sky-high by an accidental explosion during laying operations. It may be observed that there seems to have been a very general impression at this time among even the official classes at Duala that German cruisers would visit the port, and as the *Eber* and *Panther* had actually been there shortly before war was declared the supposition was they might still be lurking in the labyrinth of waterways adjoining the estuary ; as a matter of fact, however, no enemy warship made any movements in this direction throughout the operations. The only armed vessel was the *Nachtigal ;*

EUROPEAN QUARTER, DUALA

but, as will be seen, the enemy constructed spar-torpedoes to be used from small launches. They had a special inducement to prevent Duala falling into our hands, as it had been used as a refuge for all their merchantmen on the African routes, including several Woërmann liners, a Hamburg-Amerika steamer, and the *Kamerun* already mentioned, and the masts and funnels of these vessels could be seen from the base in the creeks above Duala, where they had assembled under orders from Berlin, insurance against war risks being impossible in Germany, though they could easily have escaped to Brazil long before the arrival of our warships. Their crews numbering about 400 white men were organised for service ashore in defence of the Colony.

The natives in the Duala neighbourhood were extremely disaffected towards German authority and openly expressed British sympathies, as a result of which several chiefs were hanged in the early days of August. The diary of a German officer who was in Duala which fell into our hands gives a graphic picture of life in that town in the days preceding its capture. A significant entry under date 8th August reads : " In the afternoon Rudolph Bell (a member of the royal family of Duala) and Negro

KING BELL'S PALACE. KING OF THE DUALA

Din hanged before the prison for high treason. Great outcry among the populace all night. The Dualas leaving the town in crowds." And another entry under 8th September referring to the landing of bluejackets at Victoria : " The British were led at Victoria by two Duala rascals. A reward of 1000 marks has been put on each of their heads. All canoe traffic in the creeks is stopped. Forty-eight Dualas have been captured by the patrols and brought up for judgment ; eight are to be hanged." To maintain order in the surrounding country and to bend the native population to the Imperial will, a policy of terrorism appears to have been resorted to ;

numbers of villages were pillaged and burnt and the burnings were accompanied by wholesale executions. The effect of this ruthlessness was to accentuate the sympathy of the natives for the British cause and on the arrival of the *Cumberland* and *Dwarf* there was no lack of pilots, guides, and spies ready and willing to help us. In Duala we discovered traces of frightfulness in the form of photographs too unpleasant to describe.

" Guns Q.F.C." tells us that the friendliness or otherwise of the Cameroon natives was a matter always worth considering before planning expeditions and sometimes special efforts were made to ensure their assistance. It happened that a famous brand of tempting tinned tripe formed a part of the *Cumberland's* stores, which appealed to the native palate, and on one occasion an armed launch under a naval officer was proceeding up a river to act as guardship off a small town occupied by our troops. His orders were to enlist the friendship of the local tribesmen, thereby preventing information of his movements filter-

A FEATHERED CHIEF

ing through to the Germans further inland. With this object in view he invited the chief of the tribe on board and regaled him with the delicacy referred to ; it acted like magic ! Such mutual goodwill was established that the chief insisted on presenting his host with seven wives, an offer, which for diplomatic reasons, was accepted. As time was an object and the prospective guardship was still seven miles from her station, it was decided that the good ladies should be sent by road ; their failure to appear on board at the appointed time is attributed to the vigilance of the soldiers, who placed double sentries on all posts along the road by which the " wives " were expected to travel !

Captain Fuller's task was to prepare the way for the military expedition and in this connection the importance of the Lungasi or Dibamba river was evident, flowing as it did in rear of Duala ; the Midland Railway, one of the main avenues of retreat open to the enemy, crossed it by the Yapoma bridge, and it was apparent that the threat of a landing in this direction would cause him some uneasiness. In fact, to give security from attack by enemy craft and at the same time to deny him the use of this invaluable water communication, a thorough reconnaissance of all the waterways flanking the estuary was imperative.

On 10th September the *Cumberland's* picket-boat and steam-pinnace went up the Lungasi as far as Pitti, which is on a bluff, and commands a bend in the river some seven miles from its mouth. Here the Germans had constructed a strong entrenched post which was connected by telephone with Duala. On their passage up river our boats sank a large launch, the crew of which escaped through the mangroves, followed by valedictory messages from our Maxims, but we failed on this occasion to discover an entrance to Doctor Creek, and when off Pitti were met by heavy rifle-fire which, however, was soon silenced by the picket-boats' 3 pdrs. which also drove the enemy from the entrenchments. After our landing-party had destroyed the telephones the boats returned to the base. Meanwhile the *Dwarf* with the *Balbus* and *Walrus* had successfully passed round the sunken ships and swept the channel to within about six miles of Duala without discovering any mines.

On this day (10th September) Captain Fuller was informed that the cruiser *Challenger* was on her way to assist in the landing operations, and it was evident that a channel would have to be cleared through the sunken ships to enable her to pass through and carry out an effective bombardment. It having been discovered that two additional steamers were sunk by the enemy during the previous night, the *Dwarf*, to prevent a recurrence of this, anchored near the barrage. On 11th September the main channel was swept to within three miles of Duala. While supporting the sweepers the *Dwarf* sighted a lighter in tow of a launch coming out of Mungo Creek and opened fire. This fire was returned from the hitherto silent battery at Yoss Point and the *Dwarf* was hit under the bridge, the quartermaster at the wheel being killed and five bluejackets wounded, and as the force of the battery was unknown it was decided after replying to withdraw again to the barrage.

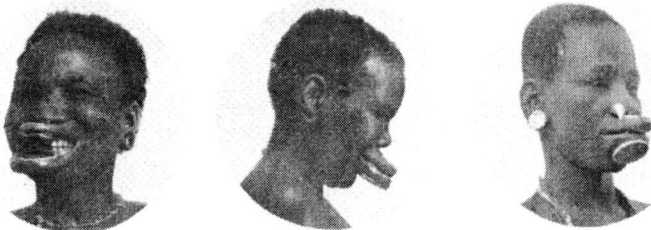

SOME OF THE WIVES !

At slack-water on the 11th the divers carried out a preliminary examination of the sunken vessels and next day the task of clearing a passage for the *Challenger* was commenced, the work being much impeded by strong currents. It was discovered that the sluice valves of the ships were open and in some cases holes knocked in the sides. To close the valves necessitated a descent into the engine-room, a proceeding involving considerable danger to the divers owing to the possibility of severing the air-pipes on the sharp edges of the wreckages. To add to the difficulty the water inside the engine-rooms was black with oil, which made the task of attending the divers a most unpleasant one.

During the night of 12th–13th September the *Ivy*,

which had temporarily relieved the *Dwarf*, was attacked by an unknown vessel which fired several shots at her from the direction of Modeaka Bay. In the darkness nothing could be seen but the flashes of the guns. The shooting was wild and no damage was done, but the incident proved the presence of armed craft in the Western Creeks which had not yet been reconnoitred. Therefore on the 14th the picket-boat, with Lieutenant Dalrymple-Hamilton, R.N., in command, and the *Vigilant* were ordered to proceed via Modeaka Bay and examine Mikanye Creek, taking care not to become seriously engaged with large vessels. The boats passed over the bay and through Mboka Creek without incident, but on emerging into Mikanye sighted an enemy launch which steamed away at high speed chased by the picket-boat until she turned into a backwater. Rounding the point which concealed the channel the picket-boat suddenly came upon the *Nachtigal* getting under way ; she at once opened fire and gave chase, the picket-boat and the *Vigilant* in this case becoming the hares ! A running fight ensued, but by forcing on every ounce of steam and making snake-like courses our boats escaped undamaged and returned to the shelter of the *Cumberland's* guns at the base. On receipt of the news the *Ivy* was at once despatched to search for the *Nachtigal*, but owing to low water was unable to get into the Bimbia river into which the enemy appeared to have withdrawn.

During these happenings of the 14th the *Dwarf*, which had again relieved the *Ivy* and had been covering the work of demolition, remained at anchor off Modeaka Bay for the night 14th–15th. At about midnight an approaching vessel was observed on which fire was opened, after which it disappeared. At daylight a large deserted steam-launch was seen aground, while a German was clinging to one of the sunken vessels making signals of distress. When removed from his perilous perch and the launch had been salved, it was discovered that a remarkably enterprising attempt had been made to sink the *Dwarf*. Two large gas cylinders, each filled with 200 lbs. of dynamite and fitted with detonators, were attached to the bow of the launch below the water-line in such a manner as to be exploded on striking any solid object. The desperado selected to steer the boat was to leap overboard at the last moment before impact. He appears, however, to have over-estimated his resolution, for when the *Dwarf* opened fire he took to the water, leaving helm on the launch which ran harmlessly into the mud, much to the disgust of the Duala Assistant Harbour Master (Lieutenant Phoëlig), who had devised the scheme.

The daring fellow proved to be a Missionary, and when questioned declared : " I am a soldier first and a Missionary second." Quite so, for during the course of the campaign we came across a number of these " Militant Missionaries " who appeared to use the rifle and Bible at discretion to suit the situation.

CAPTAIN C. H. DINNEN, THE KING'S REGIMENT, ADJUTANT WEST AFRICAN REGIMENT 1912–14, WHO WAS KILLED IN ACTION, CAMEROONS, 3.3.1915

It was now decided to investigate thoroughly the Western Creeks, and on 16th September the *Dwarf* was ordered to the Bimbia river to examine the German settlement of Tiko, ascertain the nature of its defence, and if possible bring the *Nachtigal* to action and wipe her off the slate. Piloted by the captured launch she proceeded across Mokushu Bay and passing through the Mikanye and Matumal Creeks entered the Bimbia river. Here Commander Strong turned seaward to examine the bays and inlets in the direction of Cape Bimbia, but finding no signs of enemy activity he turned inland again towards Tiko, anchoring for the night at about 5.30 p.m. five miles north-east of Sheiss Island, all lights extinguished, cable ready for slipping, and guns manned. The position of the *Nachtigal* at this time is uncertain. She seems to have been lying somewhere to the eastward of the Bimbia river and to have received information that the *Dwarf* was steaming towards Tiko, and her Captain, thinking he could get ahead, decided to conceal his ship in a small backwater and ram the *Dwarf* when she appeared next morning. He therefore after dark proceeded up the Bimbia river, not realising he was actually following his adversary. At 8.50 p.m. the *Dwarf*, sighting a light on the port bow, promptly switched on her searchlight, revealing the *Nachtigal* moving to her doom. Though apparently taken completely by surprise she at once increased to full speed in an effort to ram, whereupon the British gunboat opened a withering fire, literally blowing the *Nachtigal's* foremost gun and crew into the water, then slipping her cable she was just on the turn when she was rammed. The shock was severe, but being partially glancing the vessels separated ; the *Nachtigal*, a blazing wreck, drifted round a point of land where she blew up, while the *Dwarf* was placed alongside the river bank severely damaged, one compartment being flooded. She was patched up and returned next morning to the base with a heavy list, showing a clean cut in the side from upper deck to six feet below water-line. She was anchored in shallow water and immediately taken in hand by the *Cumberland's* engine-room staff. Within a week she was perfectly seaworthy, a piece of work of which all concerned were justifiably proud. Four Germans and ten natives who had jumped overboard from the *Nachtigal* were picked up, the remainder of the crew, including ten Germans,

CAMEROON ESTUARY, SHOWING WHERE THE " NACHTIGAL " RAMMED THE " DWARF "

perished with their ship. A few words of unstinted praise are due to the brave and resolute Commander and crew of this small vessel who, against overwhelming odds and with no hope of escape, sought out and rammed a British gunboat in these confined waterways.

The destruction of the *Nachtigal* enabled our small craft to continue to investigate the various inland waterways. On 17th September the seaward entrance to the Bimbia river was examined and an enemy launch sunk in Dikulu Bay. On the way in several Germans had been observed working on the plantations near Klippen's Point, and as they were apparently unarmed and harmless settlers they were not molested; however, on the return journey when our boats' crew were sheltering from a rain-storm, a heavy fire was opened at short range from the dense bush surrounding the plantations. Fortunately there were no casualties and a few rounds from our 3 pdr. silenced the fire, besides setting fire to the farmhouse. This incident showed the necessity for treating every German sighted as an active enemy.

PADDLE-TUG " PORPOISE " ARMED WITH 12 PDRS. FROM H.M.S. " CUMBERLAND "

On the 18th Captain Fuller ordered a reconnaissance of the Mungo Creek with a view to a possible landing at or near Bonaberi, the northern railway terminus. The enterprise was unsuccessful, for passing through a connecting channel our boat struck a submerged tree, putting her propeller out of gear. Next day, however (19th), a steam-pinnace, under Lieutenant Adams, R.N., achieved the desired end and on the return journey ran into two hostile launches, both of which she sank. One of these boats had a spar-torpedo fitted similar to that used against the *Dwarf,* and among the captives was its inventor, Lieutenant Phoëlig.

On 20th September Lieutenant Commander Sneyd again went up the Lungasi and, successfully passing through Olga Creek to the main channel, took his boat that night to within a few hundred yards of Duala. On 22nd September the redoubtable picket-boat was again sent to Mungo Creek, but, finding the enemy had thrown up lines of entrenchment at Boadibo she was, after a short engagement, forced to retire, Lieutenant Adams and some seamen being wounded.

COLONEL J. P. LAW, D.S.O., DEVONSHIRE REGIMENT AND WEST AFRICAN REGIMENT

Meanwhile the work of making a channel through the obstruction for the *Challenger* had been pressed on, though constantly impeded by foul weather and strong tides. On 18th September the survey and buoyage of the main channel being completed the actual demolition commenced, and by the 22nd the sunken vessels had been sufficiently destroyed to permit a ship of nineteen feet draught to pass through. This work called for skill and endurance on the part of the divers and their attendants, as heavy mines containing 500 lbs. of gelignite had to be

I

placed in very confined spaces in the submerged lighters during the short intervals when diving was possible. The enemy guns at Yoss Point were still unaccounted for, and the experience gained on 11th September showed it was inadvisable to expose the small vessels such as mine-sweepers, etc., to their fire, and this fact seems to have been taken advantage of by the enemy who, it was discovered, had laid some forty of their improvised mines between Yoss and Doctor Points.

On 16th September the large screw-tug *Remus* arrived from Lagos and was armed with three of the *Cumberland's* 12 pdrs., and on 22nd September the paddle-tug *Porpoise* arrived to be similarly equipped.

In addition to the reconnaissance and work described in this chapter, the flotilla was constantly engaged in patrolling the coast and other miscellaneous services too numerous to describe in detail. The *Kamerun* was salved undamaged and was soon in running order as an accommo-dation ship for prisoners of war.

Thus, by the evening of 22nd September, the result of the naval operations conducted under Captain Fuller's orders were that the whole system of inland waterways had been thoroughly reconnoitred and surveys made of those channels likely to be useful in the forthcoming landing of troops ; the only armed enemy vessel of any importance destroyed ; numerous armed launches sunk or captured with their crews ; a secure base established for the flotilla, transports, and ships of war ; a nineteen-feet channel cleared and buoyed to within 5000 yards of Duala ; direct communication established by cable with Lagos and London ; all available ships' guns mounted on the flotilla and a thorough appreciation of the situation made and despatched to Lagos to meet the General Commanding the Expeditionary Force.

All this most necessary work had been accomplished with few action casualties and without the loss of a single boat ; on the other hand, malarial fever gripped the crews of the various ships engaged, Europeans and natives alike.

In dealing with all this preliminary naval work it may appear that apparently trivial affairs have been treated in unnecessary detail, at the same time it should be remembered that the minor tactics of the struggle waged among the creeks and swamps of the estuary must be of some interest, because the Navy is liable in the future to be called in to take part in

COMMANDANT'S HOUSE, MORA (PRE-WAR)

similar expeditions against savage or semi-civilised adversaries, or indeed against European Powers having tropical possessions.

Before describing the arrival of the Expeditionary Force it will be as well to refer briefly to the military operations undertaken by the " Waffs " on the Nigerian-Cameroon border. It will be remembered that Colonel Carter, the Commandant of the Nigerian forces, had been anxious to invade German territory by land, but that the

Home authorities did not consider it desirable to initiate an offensive prior to the arrival of the Allied Expeditionary Force under General Dobell at Duala. On 14th August permission had been granted through the Acting Governor to reconnoitre the frontier, subject to the troops not becoming involved in serious hostilities. Rather a difficult position for the Commandant, for had the enemy invaded Nigeria in force, he would have had no choice. It would have been a fight to a finish. However, be that as it may, the rôle of the frontier columns for the present was to be one of local activity, the chief object being to gain information and distract the enemy's attention from the main objective, Duala.

What actually happened was this : about 24th August Headquarters at Lagos apparently ordered an immediate advance. The northern column was to seize Mora, the Yola column to occupy Garua, and the Cross river column was to advance on Nsanakang, about five miles beyond the frontier. Unfortunately, for various reasons unnecessary to pursue, the operations thus initiated were from the outset attended by misfortune. The northern or Maidugari column, having crossed the frontier on 25th August, encountered an enemy force in an almost impregnable position in the mountains near Mora, whence it failed to dislodge them, and after suffering many casualties, on 27th August it was forced to retire, taking up a position to the south of Mora with the object of preventing the enemy there from joining hands with the Garua garrison ; at about the same time an unsuccessful attack was also made by a French column from Fort Lamy, on the north-eastern frontier, on Kusseri, the principal German post in that region.

The Yola column crossed the frontier on 25th August and the Mounted Infantry, after a sharp combat and suffering heavy casualties, drove the enemy from the village of Tepe. The British column then resumed its march on Garua, which place was attacked on the night of 30th–31st August. This attack failed, and after sustaining severe losses the whole force was compelled to fall back on Yola and adopt a strictly defensive attitude.

On 2nd September the Governor General, Sir Frederick Lugard, arrived at Lagos from England, and on his recommendation Brigadier General F. J. Cunliffe, C.B., C.M.G., then reorganising the Yola column, was appointed to command the Nigerian forces.

Still worse news was to come, for on 6th September the Cross river column holding Nsanakang was suddenly attacked by a superior German force, and notwithstanding

FORT KUSSERI, CAPTURED BY THE FRENCH, 00.19

a most gallant resistance was practically annihilated, only two officers and some ninety native soldiers escaping by forcing their way through the enemy with the bayonet. The German losses were even heavier than our own— a redeeming feature of the fight.

This reverse was rather serious, because the victorious Germans were in a position to threaten Calabar and the Niger delta, and in order to restore the situation troops and guns had to be detached from the force which had been concentrated for General Dobell's Duala expedition, and a purely defensive attitude adopted along the whole frontier.

These early inland frontier adventures attended by ill-luck and so uniformly unsuccessful, though not in accordance with the intentions of the Colonial Office, undoubtedly shook the enemy, caused him many casualties, and for the time being considerably weakened his forces in other regions.

It is remarkable how quickly the natives of Sierra Leone knew of these reverses, thousands of miles away. General Daniell, Commanding the Troops in Sierra Leone, received the news by cypher telegram, but the natives knew of it before the receipt of the telegram. Could it have been conveyed to them by drum signals ?

CHAPTER VII

FORMATION OF THE EXPEDITIONARY FORCE—ITS CONCENTRATION AT
SUELLABA—OPERATION IN THE LUNGASI RIVER—SURRENDER OF
DUALA—SITUATION FOLLOWING THE SURRENDER—CLEARING THE
NEIGHBOURHOOD

HARKING back to Chapter IV we know that General Dobell and Staff sailed from Liverpool in the Elder-Dempster liner *Appam* on 31st August, 1914. Let us now follow him down the African coast and see how he gathered his Allied black battalions and guided them through nearly eighteen months of warfare, neither sanguinary nor sensational in the modern sense and bearing no comparison with the battle of giants being waged in Europe ; nevertheless, strenuous, sweltering, nerve-shaking, and, above all, successful ; commencing with the amphibious phase with its accompanying mud baths, continuing and ending with the bush, plain, mountain and forest business.

Escorted by H.M.S. *Challenger* (Captain C. P. Beaty-Pownall), the first port of call was Bathurst, at the mouth of the Gambia river, the oldest British possession in Africa. Here on the 10th September a detachment of the Gambia Company of the " Waffs " was embarked. Then passing southwards, the harbour of Sierra Leone was entered on 12th September. Here the French contingent of the Expeditionary Force from Dakar in five transports with the cruiser *Bruix*, 5000 tons (Commandant de Vaisseau M. E. Tirard), had assembled.

During August and the early days of September we, in Sierra Leone, had been preparing a contingent of troops—Infantry, Artillery, and Royal Engineers with a Carrier Corps, supplies, etc., for service with General

Dobell's expedition, and considerable quantities of ammunition—gun and small-arm—had already been despatched to the Gold Coast and Nigeria.

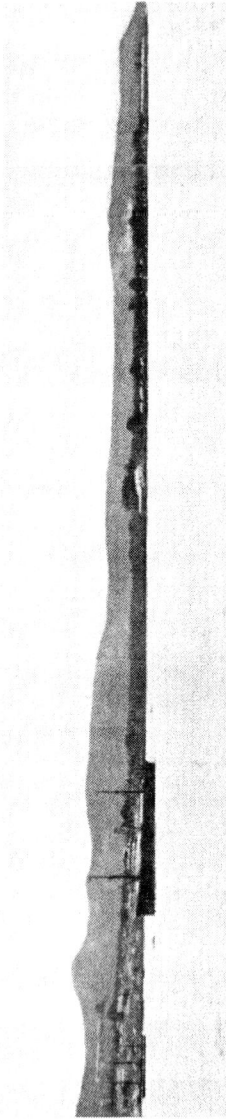

It was about this time that the big German liner *Professor Woërmann* was captured in the Atlantic, brought into Freetown harbour and there adjudged a prize of war, the first time such an event had occurred for over a hundred years. When taken, she was loaded to the gunwales with all kinds of good things from the Fatherland. Expensive cameras and photographic accessories, scents, sweetmeats, soap, cloth, lager beer, Rhine wines, and many other luxuries, together with a large consignment of postage stamps destined for the Cameroons. These stamps proved most useful, being eventually surcharged with the letters C.E.F. (Cameroon Expeditionary Force) and postally used by the Allies following the occupation of Duala. Those surcharged are now much coveted by philatelists. But the most useful and opportune find on this ship from a military point of view was a mass of new maps of the Cameroons, which were duly transferred to General Dobell's staff aboard the *Appam*.

The approximate strength and composition of the

Courtesy of Lisk Carew.

DISTANT PANORAMA OF SIERRA LEONE PENINSULA. FREETOWN ON LEFT, WILBERFORCE HILL EXTREME RIGHT

Sierra Leone contingent embarked on 13th September was :—

West African Regiment: 40 British officers and non-commissioned officers, 700 native ranks under Lieut. Col. E. Vaughan.

Sierra Leone R.G.A.: 5 British officers and non-commissioned officers, 50 native ranks, and 4 guns under Captain N. D. A. Fitzgerald.

Field Section R.E. under Lieutenant C. V. S. Jackson. Also Medical, Ordnance, and Transport Officers with

WEST AFRICAN REGIMENT EMBARKING, 13.9.1914

a Carrier Corps and plentiful supplies of ammunition, stores, and food.

On receipt of the embarkation order there was much rejoicing by those who had drawn lucky numbers, and there was not a little weeping and gnashing of teeth by those destined to remain behind. But in soldiering, " 'tis ever thus ! " Some must go—some must stay—and the " stayers " tear their hearts out in the staying, and in the hour of departure when the troops are on parade, and the order to march is given and the colours fly, and the brave drums beat, and the valorous bugles sing, and the soldiers cheer lustily, and the "stayers" behold through filmy eyes the light-hearted mirth of the campaigners in the making—then does the iron enter into their soul. But listen ! The stay-behinds of to-day became the heroes of to-morrow, for they did not comprehend in this their hour of disappointment that in the long years of strife and anguish to be, they would sooner or later be gathered into the seething cauldron, in which they would have their fill of fighting, and many a good deal more than that.

Having drawn what I suppose I may call a lucky number, and after most reluctantly taking leave of General Daniell, I joined the happy throng aboard the good ship *Appam* on the evening of 13th September, 1914, to assume command of the British contingent of the Cameroon Expeditionary Force. The *Appam* was a comfortable and well-appointed ship, a floating palace in comparison with some of her elder sisters of the same line, which leaked like sieves when bluffing the "Trades," on which the rats were called by their Christian names and the cockroaches crawled merrily round the bunks by night. Later in the war, this same *Appam* was captured off Madeira by the German auxiliary cruiser *Moewe*. She was homeward-bound and had on board a number of officials from our Coast colonies, including Sir Edward Merewether, K.C.M.G., Governor and Commander-in-Chief of Sierra Leone. She was sent to Virginia, U.S.A., and after much litigation eventually released and returned to the owners.

Escorted by the *Challenger*, we left Freetown harbour at sunset, and steaming slowly southwards, on the following day coasted Liberia, the Negro Republic sandwiched between Sierra Leone and the French colony of the Ivory Coast. Monrovia, the capital and chief port, is pleasantly situated on rising ground within the promontory of Cape Mesurada, which protects the anchorage from the full swing of the Atlantic swell, making landing operations fairly safe. With some expenditure, a good harbour could be made here, and as a matter of recent history a certain American firm, big manufacturers of tyres, having discovered an ideal spot in Liberia for rubber growing, have not only obtained concessions for something like a million acres of virgin forest, hitherto unsullied by the hand of man, but are making roads and actually constructing a harbour at Monrovia. Well !—they are welcome to everything they can find there, including the seven kinds of venomous serpents, crocodiles (three species),

Courtesy of Lisk Carew.

THE LANDING STAGE, FREETOWN. ELDER-DEMPSTER LINER
S.S. " APPAM " IN PORT

poisonous lizards, and scorpions galore—not forgetting bugs and burrowing fleas !

Coffin-making was said to be the most flourishing industry, the cemetery the show spot of Monrovia, and the road leading thereto the fashionable evening stalk of the local aristocracy.

The late Colonel Seymour Vandeleur, D.S.O., who visited Liberia in 1896, tells us that the Liberian officials of those days held a somewhat exaggerated opinion of their own importance and the influence of their country on world affairs, though their knowledge of history appeared to be rather vague, as will be gathered from the following anecdote :

A French officer, who was a passenger on board a ship which put in at Monrovia for a few hours to take in cargo, went ashore for the purpose of getting a little quiet exercise, and whilst strolling down the main street he bumped into a Liberian senator, who wrathfully turned upon him and shouted :

" You damned Frenchman ! What for you shove me ? What for we give you at Vaterloo ? "

But, *autres temps, autres mœurs.*

During the Great War Liberia joined the Allies against Germany, and on one occasion was visited by a German submarine, the crew of which boarded the only ship the Liberians possessed, a Revenue cutter. This was followed by an ultimatum to dismantle the wireless station, surrender the English Bank, and hand over all French and British colonists. In spite of their impotence the Liberian Government were true to their trust and ignored the German request. The submarine thereupon proceeded to bombard the place, killing and wounding several inhabitants, when an Elder-Dempster liner *Barutu* (Captain Yardley) suddenly appeared on the scene, engaged with the submarine, and compelled her to withdraw.

The Gold Coast was reached on 16th September, and a transport containing a portion of the Gold Coast Regiment, Infantry and Artillery, joined the convoy off Accra. Lome, the port of Togoland (now a British possession), was visited on the same day, and here a detachment of the Sierra Leone Battalion of the " Waffs," which had been despatched as a reinforcement from Sierra Leone but had arrived too late to take part in the conquest of Togoland, was embarked. On 17th September we anchored off Lagos, where the main body of the force from Nigeria, consisting of two Battalions of Infantry, a Battery of Artillery, a Carrier Corps, and a number of Medical,

Supply, and Transport Officers in four transports, joined up and completed the British contingent. Here for forty-eight hours we lay at anchor in the deep water at the edge of the surf, exposed to the full force of an ocean swell—not a very pleasant experience for those who did not love the sea. For " true sailors " it was no doubt a comforting sensation. It was fascinating to watch the white-crested rollers breaking in monotonous succession on the shallows, resembling in the distance endless lines of plumed squadrons charging in battle array up the sandy strands.

LANDING STAGE, DUALA

The British portion of the expedition left for Duala on 20th September, whilst the French, which had proceeded independently from Sierra Leone, had called at Lagos on the 18th and from there went to the Calabar river to take in supplies of food and water.

The British arrived at the Suellaba anchorage on the morning of 23rd September when General Dobell received from Captain Fuller a report of the work and progress made in preparing the way for landing operations. Mine-sweeping had been resumed that morning under cover of the *Dwarf*, and the channel, now reported clear for about two miles above the sunken vessels, was carefully surveyed and marked. During this work the enemy made no attempt to interfere with our movements, though it had been hoped that the position of the defences would be revealed, but the guns were silent.

On the arrival of the *Challenger* steps were at once taken to reduce her draught, and it was wisely decided not to attempt a landing until it was definitely ascertained that she could proceed within effective range of the town.

On the 24th a reconnaissance of the Lungasi river was carried out by Lieutenant Commander Sneyd, accompanied by Captain Howell, R.A., an officer of the H.Q. Staff. The enemy post at Pitti was found to be strongly held, and some sniping took place from Yansoki, the result of the investigations showing that the north bank of the river was quite unsuitable for landing large bodies of troops, but that small parties might be able to scramble ashore through the mangroves near Mbenge. While the Lungasi was being examined, another mile of the channel above the wrecks was swept and surveyed, and the *Dwarf* anchored for the night off Doctor Point, this position now being described as the " advanced base." The same evening the *Challenger* reported her draught as being 19 feet 7 inches, and next morning (25th) she joined the *Dwarf*. She touched bottom passing through the wreckage, but was fortunately forced through undamaged into deep water. Meanwhile, the sweepers had discovered the enemy mine-field and commenced clearing it. The French expedition having arrived this day brought the number of Allied vessels up to about thirty, including men-of-war, transports, cable ship, and the armed flotilla, all lying at anchor within the estuary—quite an imposing array, which was visible from the slopes of Cameroon mountain, and must have caused the Germans to think a bit uneasily. It was also on this date (25th) that General Dobell and Captain Fuller went on board the *Challenger* and despatched an ultimatum to the German Governor, warning him that if the Colony was not surrendered

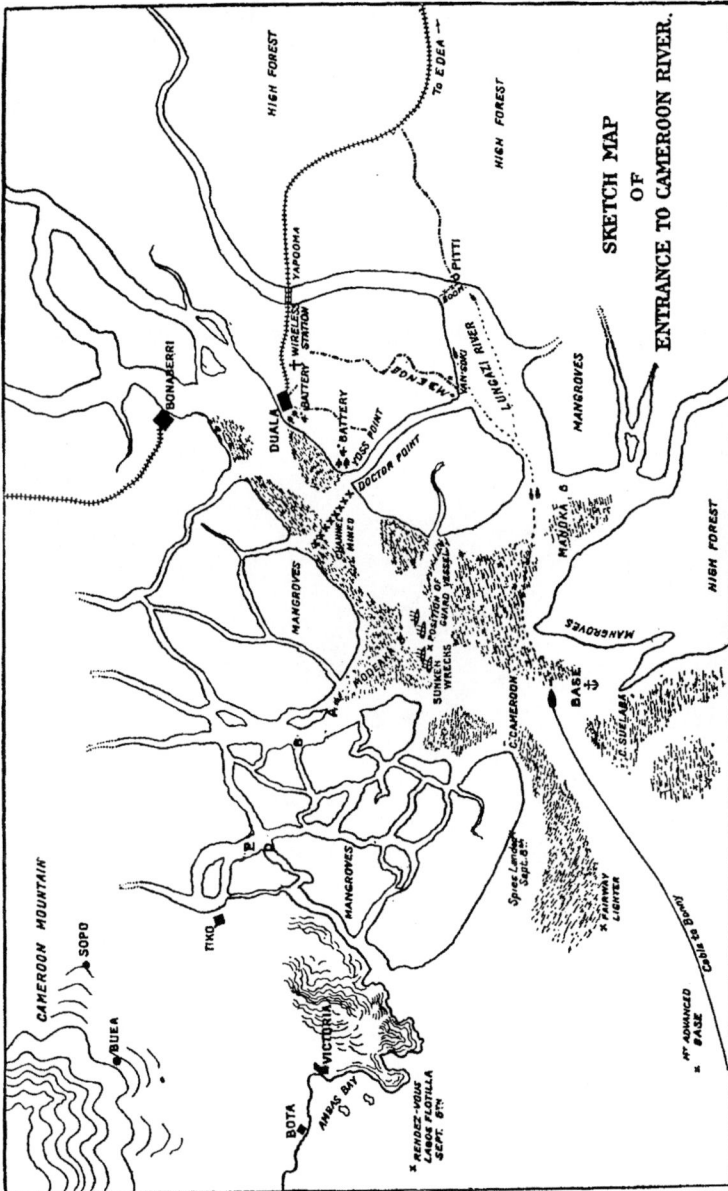

SKETCH MAP
OF
ENTRANCE TO CAMEROON RIVER.

ROUGH SKETCH TO SHOW FLANK MOVEMENT IN LUNGASI RIVER

unconditionally, Duala would be bombarded. The ultimatum was sent in a picket-boat, which was met on the way by an emissary under the white flag, and the behaviour of the Germans on receiving the message was typical.

During the two hours which had been granted for a reply our ships, of course, displayed the white flag, but shortly after the ultimatum had been received at Duala the enemy launched a number of floating mines down stream on the swift-running current. Fortunately, no

GOVERNMENT HOUSE, DUALA

damage was done, as on approaching the ships the mines were destroyed by our rifle- and machine-gun fire.

At the expiration of the period of grace allowed, the reply, couched in evasive terms, was received, containing, amongst other matters, a protest against our having opened fire whilst the white flags were flying ! but by the time the document had been fully deciphered darkness had fallen, making it impossible to commence operations until the morrow.

Following the reconnaissance of the 24th, General Dobell had decided, notwithstanding the unfavourable conditions reported, the method of attack on Duala must be a turning movement, from the Lungasi to the Midland railway, thus cutting off the enemy's retreat, whilst the *Challenger* distracted his attention by a bombardment from the Duala river. I was ordered to control the operation and, to execute the plan, it was arranged that the armed tugs *Porpoise* and *Remus* with the Pioneer Company of the Gold Coast Regiment under Captain Harvey Goodwin, should proceed up the Lungasi at daylight on the 26th, and after capturing Pitti and cutting the telephone wire, continue up stream and if possible prevent the enemy from crossing the railway bridge at Yapoma. The remainder of the troops detailed for this operation were

Courtesy of London Electrotype Agency.

THE PESTILENTIAL SWAMPS

divided into two separate detachments, the first, as a covering force, was to be carried in a small transport, the s.s. *Marina* (ex-German), and some lighters towed by the *Crocodile* and *Alligator* (most appropriate names for the work in hand, for we observed many of them basking on the flats, waiting to devour any unfortunate who might slip overboard !), and disembark on the right bank of the river in the vicinity of Mbenge. The second—the first reinforcement—in two small steamers, was to anchor at the entrance to the river until the covering force had made good its landing. The latter consisted of the West African Regiment, a section of the Sierra Leone Artillery, and a detachment of Royal Engineers under Lieut. Col.

K

Vaughan, and the first reinforcement of the 1st Battalion Nigeria Regiment with a section of Nigerian Artillery under Lieut. Col. Cockburn, the strength of each being approximately 40 officers and N.C.O.'s, 600 native ranks, and some 400 carriers, the whole under Lieut. Col. Cunliffe. The remainder of the British contingent and the French were to remain on the transports at the base and await developments. The *Challenger* at daylight opened fire with her 6-inch guns, causing some damage to property, one shell hitting Government House, but in view of the anticipated success of the military landing operation, it was not considered desirable to injure the town to any extent, the chief aim being to unsettle the enemy and shake his nerves. Consequently, the bombardment was not persisted in.

Unfortunately, the Lungasi adventure failed. The *Remus* and *Porpoise* advanced to Pitti, where they met with strong opposition. This was quickly silenced by a bombardment, and, after searching the neighbourhood with shell-fire for about an hour, the two tugs closed on Pitti and sent in a party to destroy the telephone instruments. On approaching the shore, however, the boats were received with a violent rifle- and machine-gun fire from a concealed enemy, and forced to return. It was then discovered that a boom had been placed across the river which forbade approach to the Yapoma railway bridge, and as a landing at Pitti was at present out of the question, the vessels withdrew, subjected to a heavy fire from the dense Bush on both banks as they dropped down-stream. This detachment was fortunate in the small number of its casualties, as at the close range bullets freely penetrated the light improvised armour of the tugs which were packed with men. Meanwhile a portion of the covering force had been landed near Mbenge according to plan, but the country proved to be quite impassable and the companies detached to occupy Yansoke failed to reach their objective. Accompanied by my Staff officer, Major Wallace Wright,

V.C., I proceeded at midday up the Lungasi on the launch *Vigilant* to see how things were progressing, and on arrival at the point where the troops had disembarked, we found the transport and lighters high and dry on the

1. THE FLOATING DOCK
2. GERMAN GOVERNMENT YACHT " HERTZOGIN ELIZABETH "

mud with the tide ebbing and strength and positions of enemy unknown. Officers and men were floundering in the mangrove morass, and a little further up stream we came upon Captains Keyworth and Brand, above their waists in the soupy waters making desperate efforts to keep the men in hand and lead them to terra firma.

Topsy-turvydom set in mud and slime was the impression the scene left on my mind. After a further examination of the position, and receiving verbal reports from Colonel Cunliffe and other officers, all of which pointed to the impracticability of continuing operations in such surroundings, and seeing that by exposing the native troops at the outset of a campaign to such conditions for any length of time would greatly impair their efficiency, I decided to withdraw the whole force from the river to the base as soon as the vessels could be refloated. This was accomplished, happily without casualties, by the early morning of 27th September, Headquarters approving of my action.

The only redeeming feature of the episode was that our activity in the river caused the enemy to appreciate the fact that Duala was being threatened from the rear, thus hastening his decision to evacuate and surrender the town.

It now seemed quite certain that a direct attack must be made on Duala, and early on 27th September, the General, accompanied by the Allied Commanders, proceeded in the *Ivy* to an anchorage off Bwape Sand in order to examine Yoss Point and decide on its suitability for landing troops. Whilst this matter was being discussed, our attention was arrested by a succession of violent explosions followed by the total collapse of the huge steel masts of the wireless station and the hoisting of several white flags over Government House and other prominent buildings in the town. At 11 a.m. a representative of the German Government arrived on board and agreed to surrender Duala and Bonaberi unconditionally, and in the afternoon the General, with a detachment of the *Challenger's* marines, landed and formally took possession of the town, while a detachment of bluejackets was landed at Bonaberi. The Union Jack and Tricolour were ceremoniously hoisted at Government House flagstaff, and the capital of the Cameroons passed into the hands of the Allies.

An obstruction having been found in the main channel,

it was impossible to get the transports up from the base to the landing-piers ; for the first night, therefore, both Duala and Bonaberi were held by detachments of marines and seamen from the *Challenger*, and until the channel was cleared nothing could be done to relieve the English prisoners who had been kept on board one of the German liners hidden in the creeks above the town.

There seems to be little doubt that the Germans never intended to defend Duala seriously, but to retire inland and wait for the anticipated victories of the Fatherland in Europe. As early as 10th September, the Post Office

TROOPS DISEMBARKING AT DUALA

stores were loaded on a train ready for evacuation ; the Governor left on the 25th, the Military Commandant with the native garrison on the 26th, and the reply to our ultimatum was evidently couched in evasive terms in order to gain time. Most of the railway rolling stock had been removed, the wireless station completely destroyed, and large quantities of stores, provisions, and armaments transported to the interior.

Nine large liners of the Hamburg house of Woërmann, with a total tonnage of 31,000, was the chief prize. Forty to fifty lighters, motor-boats, steam-launches, a floating dock, a shallow draught stern-wheel gunboat, a large quantity of railway and dockyard material, and a battery of field guns fell into our hands. About four hundred prisoners were taken, including a detachment of seventy armed Germans who had been left in charge of the town. The Governor's steam-yacht *Hertzogin Elizabeth* was discovered stuck in the mud, while the floating dock had been sunk. Both were raised and repaired, and proved most useful to the Navy. This completed the list of booty, the total value of which was estimated at about £3,000,000.

Until the captured merchantmen could be sent home under escort, guards had to be found to look after the valuable property they contained, and a young officer of the W.A.R. who was detailed for this duty and who made his headquarters in the Captain's cabin of the s.s. *Arnfried*, told me this little yarn : For the purpose of visiting the guards on the various ships, a steam-pinnace was placed at his disposal and the coxswain and crew were accommodated on his ship. Shortly after taking over his duties, a native chief from a village near by came aboard to pay his respects and incidentally to see what he could pick up in the " square-face " and tobacco line and " dashed " the officer a fine fat duck which he cooked in anticipation of a cold duck lunch the following day. The duck was placed on a shelf near the cabin port-hole, but the ship's cat came along and devoured it. This being its third offence, the officer was very angry and said something about the cat being destroyed. A little later the coxswain of the pinnace, a true type of the old British sailorman, but without any previous experience of the coast, came to the officer's cabin in a great state of excitement and reported : " Beggin' yer pardin, sir, but that there ship's cat as you said you'd 'ave done in, is now 'anging over the galley fire with all 'is fur on and your troops all buzzin' around like a swarm of bees awaiting till 'es cooked, all ready to heat 'im like." He didn't understand that cats, rats, lizards, and snakes were favourite articles of diet to the Mendi tribesmen, and that roasting them whole as soon as they are killed makes them all the more tasty.

The loss of Duala had gravely compromised the prestige

of the Germans among the natives of the coast region, and
Herr Ebermaier felt it necessary to make some counter-
stroke. In a circular letter to the officials concerned, the
Governor wrote that, as the loss of Duala could not be
concealed, and as " damaging perversions and exaggera-
tions " would be the result if the circulation of the news
was left to native gossip, administrative officers were
authorised to announce the fact in a form " suited to the
circumstances of each district." Lest they should be in

THE KAISERHOF, RENAMED THE " GEORGE INN "

doubt as to the suitable form, the lines upon which the
publication should be made were put forward by the
Governor himself—a masterpiece in the art of invention.

As the terms of capitulation only included the towns
of Duala and Bonaberi and their immediate vicinity, it was
evident there could be no security for a shore base until
the surrounding country had been cleared of the enemy,
whose strength was still uncertain. It was therefore
essential to widen the perimeter. On 28th September the
troops were landed and allotted to their various sections
of defence on both banks of the river, whilst the naval

authorities took stock of their captured acquisitions. The *Challenger* and *Dwarf* anchored in the stream off the town ; the *Cumberland* and the French warships remaining at Suellaba base.

General Headquarters were established in Government House and British Headquarters in a comfortable residence opposite the " Kaiserhof" (renamed the " George Inn "), in which was discovered a large tank which in German days overflowed with lager beer. Bismarck once said : " Das Bier ist ein zeittöter " (Beer is a time-killer), but in this particular instance we didn't find it so, for the Germans had left sufficient only to enable us Britishers to slake a glorious tropical thirst—a matter of a few moments only.

On the 29th the Yapoma bridge was again reconnoitred by land and water, when it was found that two spans had been destroyed and that the enemy was in force on the opposite bank.

From information received at this time it appeared that the Germans had retired in three directions, viz. to Jabassi on the Wuri river, to Edea on the Sanaga and up the Northern railway, and that detachments were scattered about the creeks of the estuary and on Buea mountain.

The disembarkation of the troops was completed by 30th September, on which date two flotillas, each carrying 150 men of the West African Regiment, were despatched through the creeks to deal with enemy detachments reported to be holding Tiko on the Bimbia river and Missellelle plantation, north of Mowe Lake. The Tiko party, after a sharp encounter, dislodged the enemy from that place and drove them towards Buea, their Commander being killed. The other seized Missellelle, took thirteen German prisoners, and secured a large stock of provisions, badly needed in Duala at that time.

The 2nd Battalion Nigeria Regiment under Lieut. Col. A. H. W. Haywood, having occupied Bonaberi, commenced to advance along the Northern railway towards

Maka, encountering considerable opposition. Meanwhile the French had met with strong resistance at Yapoma bridge and had to be reinforced.

During the early days of October the country was further examined in all directions, the most important reconnaissance being made up the Wuri river by Commander Strong in the captured stern-wheel gunboat,

1. YAPOMA BRIDGE AFTER DESTRUCTION BY ENEMY
2. OUR TROOPS CROSSING LUNGASI RIVER ON RAFTS

renamed *Sokoto*. On the 3rd and 4th, he penetrated as far as Jabassi, fifty miles above Duala, where he reconnoitred strongly held positions and gained much valuable information. He likewise investigated the Abo, a tributary of the Wuri, reaching Miang, twenty miles from Duala, and after destroying telephone communications there, returned to Headquarters. On the 5th, a flotilla carried out a reconnaissance up the Mungo creek, found enemy strongly entrenched at Bunyo (thirteen miles from Duala), and after a sharp engagement drove them inland.

We know that on 1st October the French were held up at Yapoma. On the 2nd, a detachment of Marines and Engineers was landed at Pitti from the *Remus*, hoping to outflank the Germans and cut the railway behind them, but this effort to relieve the situation failed, the bush being so dense and swampy and enemy so well concealed

Courtesy of Illustrated London News.

FRENCH SENEGALESE TROOPS STORMING THE YAPOMA BRIDGE, 6.10.1914

that no progress could be made. The men were therefore re-embarked and returned to their ships.

It now became necessary to plan a more elaborate operation, viz. to force a passage by a direct crossing combined with a strong turning movement from the left bank. Accordingly, on 5th October, the *Cumberland* and *Challenger's* field guns were sent up the line to assist the French Artillery, which was of very light calibre, whilst four hundred *tirailleurs* were landed at Pitti from a flotilla of small craft, and a number of surf-boats and barges were held in readiness to carry the main body across the river. Unfortunately, the turning movement again failed, the troops in spite of tremendous efforts being unable to make headway through such appalling, impenetrable country under sustained machine-gun fire.

At last, on 6th October, a direct attack succeeded.

Following a heavy bombardment, a passage was forced by the brave Senegalese troops who, under a galling fire, swarmed over the broken girders of the bridge, while the remainder, crossing in the surf-boats and barges, carried the position, thus finally securing Duala from possible attacks from the eastward and paving the way for an advance on Edea, whither the Germans had retired. Investigations further afield were undertaken by the *Ivy*. On 1st October she appeared off Victoria, and her Captain, finding no enemy troops there, proceeded to Fernando Po to inform the Spanish Governor of the fall of Duala. This mission accomplished, he went to the mouth of the Sanaga river, some Germans trekking inland as the ship approached. The natives, however, appeared to be quite friendly and reported plenty of water in the river for light draught vessels, so with this and other useful information, Commander Hughes returned to Duala on 6th October.

CHAPTER VIII

INFORMATION received by General Dobell from various sources at this stage went to show that there were two main concentrations of enemy troops in the coastal region, one at Jabassi up the Wuri river, the other at Edea where the Midland railway crosses the Sanaga, and it was apparent that, before our occupation of Duala could be considered secure, it would be necessary to defeat or drive back these forces.

Though Jabassi and Edea were approximately equidistant from Duala, an offensive against the former was an easier undertaking than against the latter, the Wuri river providing good water communication in the wet season, while the road to Edea ran through very difficult country—bush, forest, and swamp. There was an additional inducement to expedite the attack on Jabassi in the fact that the rainy season was drawing to its close, when the rivers would fall and render navigation impossible except for small launches. So it happened that on 6th October, when the French had with difficulty stormed the Yapoma bridge, an expedition composed of a small mixed naval and military force, the command of which General Dobell entrusted to me, was in readiness to strike at Jabassi. The naval detachment under Lieutenant Commander the Hon. B. T. C. O. Freeman-Mitford of H.M.S. *Challenger*, who also commanded the flotilla, consisted of 100 seamen and Marines, two 6-inch naval guns, and a 12 pdr. field gun with the gun crews. The military detachment under Lieut. Col. Vaughan included

four mountain guns, six companies West Africans, two
companies 1st Nigerians, the Pioneer Company Gold Coast
Regiment, and some 600 carriers.

The flotilla in which this force was stowed away was
made up of all manner of light craft (many of them
captured), including a small coasting vessel, a dredger, six

SKETCH OF WURI RIVER TO JABASSI

steam-launches of various shapes and sizes, two 100-feet
motor-launches, a steam-tug, a stern-wheeler, eight steel
lighters, eight surf-boats, a motor-pinnace, a steam ditto,
and the *Cumberland's* picket-boat (*The Red Devil*). Two of
this motley assemblage deserve special mention, viz. the
dredger *Mole* and one of the steel lighters, for on these
were mounted the 6-inch guns from the *Challenger*, the

former being semi-officially christened the *Iron Duke*, the
latter, *Dreadnought*, by the Senior Service. This tickled
the fancy of the soldiers, who perceived in these craft an
ingenious innovation, indicating intelligence in the inventor. They were, in fact, river monitors.

The orders were to seize Jabassi and attack any hostile
force in its vicinity. The embarkation was completed at
Duala by the evening of the 6th, and at 5.30 a.m., on
7th October, the flotilla, like some huge sea monster
moving in from the deep, forged its way up the winding
and swiftly-running Wuri, its pilot fish the picket-boat.
The river on both banks was nothing but an impenetrable
tangle of dense Bush and high elephant grass. Just before
sundown we were fired on from Nsake Hill, about ten
miles below Jabassi on the left bank. This fire was
quickly silenced by the 3 pdrs. and Maxims of the leading
craft, and Nsake was occupied by a company of the West
Africans ; a detachment was also landed on the opposite
bank and the flotilla, covered by these troops, anchored
for the night in midstream. We weighed at dawn on the
8th, and moving slowly onward at 7 a.m., reached a
point in the bend of the river about three miles below and
in view of Jabassi, perched on high ground on the right
bank.

The expediency of advancing up both banks of the
river was now carefully considered, but in the absence of
definite information as to the enemy's strength, and in
view of the denseness of the undergrowth on the left bank,
which in places was intersected by impassable swamps,
I decided to keep the troops intact on the right until the
situation became more clearly defined. I was, in fact,
very loath to throw a portion of my small force into such
a blind piece of unknown country—cut off as it would
have been by the river, and liable to be trapped by
superior numbers. Consequently, we drew up alongside
the right bank, and completing the disembarkation by
9 a.m., the force moved forward with two companies as

Courtesy of The Sphere.

1. DREADNOUGHT

2. WURI RIVER AT JABASSI

advance and left flank guards, five companies and a section of mountain guns main body, while two companies, the naval detachment and 12 pdr. gun, were held in reserve.

A muddy pathway through dense elephant grass running parallel with and close to the river was followed, and our right was protected by the armed flotilla. By 10.30 a.m. the main body had reached a hillock (A) about three-quarters of a mile from the town. This hillock had been prepared for defence and strongly entrenched, but had been recently evacuated by the Germans, and at this point, on information gathered from scouts, three companies were detached to the left to try a turning movement against the enemy main position, which had been located on what they called Government Hill, just above the town, but the country was so dense that cohesion was practically impossible. The moment troops were launched forth they were lost to sight. It was a case of " Follow my leader and trust to luck ! " Whilst this flank movement was in progress, Lieut. Col. Vaughan advanced up the river bank to attack the position in front. At 11.30 a.m. the reserve with the 12 pdr. gun was ordered up to the hillock (A) on which we had now established Headquarters.

As these troops were closing on the hill, a sudden burst of machine-gun and rifle-fire was opened upon them and on the flotilla, which was steaming slowly up stream, conforming to the general movement. This fire, directed from the Bush on the left bank, though heavy, was a bit wild, and did little damage to the troops, but it was remarkable that at such close range the boats' crews were not wiped out, for bullets were literally rained upon them. The fire was replied to by every gun and rifle that could bear, but as the enemy was invisible no effect could be observed, and at about 1 p.m., the boats, being in a somewhat critical position, were ordered to drop down to a bend in the river. Unfortunately, the tug *Balbus*, towing the

Dreadnought, ran aground on a small island and had to be abandoned. The coolness displayed by Commander Mitford and the crews of the various craft under this hail

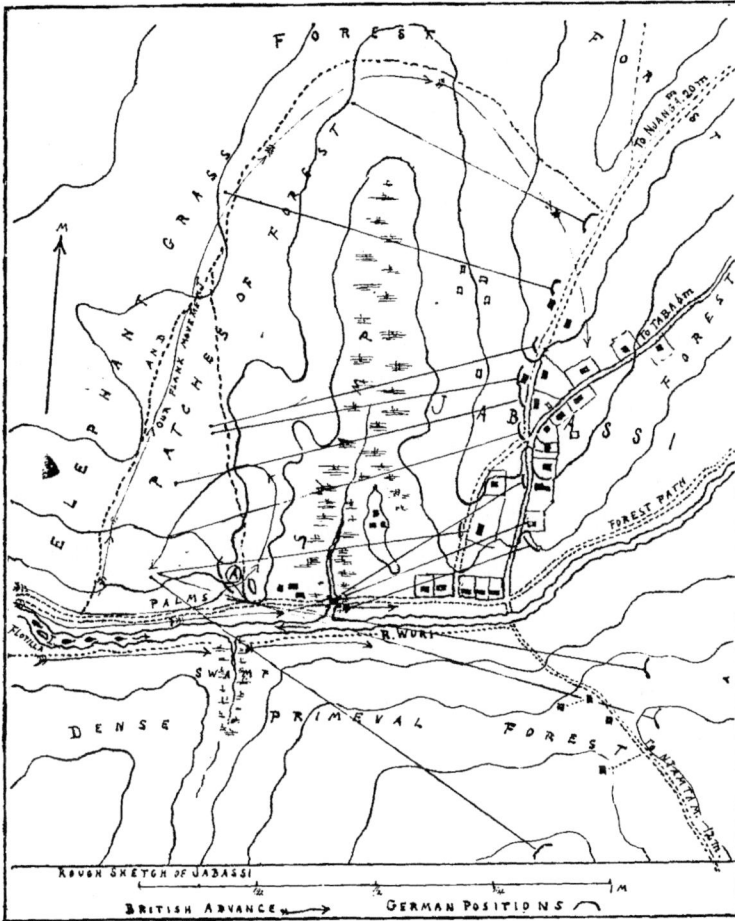

ROUGH SKETCH OF JABASSI

of bullets, which we soldiers witnessed from the bank, was most heartening to all.

Lieut. Col. Vaughan, with the main body, had now (1.30 p.m.) reached a clearing in the Bush and occupied some tin buildings on the river bank about eight hundred

L

yards from the enemy main position. Here, however, he was subjected to a most severe cross fire from concealed machine-guns, and finding an unfordable swamp in his immediate front, he evacuated the buildings and moved to an opening to his left, hoping to find a way through, but here also he was confronted with a similar situation and could make no progress. At about 2 p.m. I went forward with my Staff officers. We found the troops suffering from the effects of the terrific heat, tactical unity completely lost in the dense elephant grass through which officers were trying to lead the men, many of whom showed signs of hanging back under the constant bursts of machine-gun fire, of which this was their first experience. Reinforcements were then brought up with the object of gaining a footing beyond a small bridge spanning the swamp, but as this effort proved unavailing, I turned to that portion of the reserve in which I had placed so much reliance, viz. the naval detachment. To my surprise, and disappointment, I found the men completely prostrated and incapable of further action, caused through their exertions in dragging the 12 pdr. gun over the mud track and up to the hill position under the blazing sun. At the same moment a message was brought in to say the flank movement was held up.

It now became evident that Jabassi was not destined to fall into our hands on this day, and as the sun was casting long shadows I decided to re-embark the troops. A retirement was therefore ordered to the morning position, where the re-embarkation was carried out under circumstances of some difficulty, fortunately without molestation, and the flotilla in the darkness dropped down stream and anchored off Nsake after an exciting passage during which the strong current, some bumps, uncharted shoals, floating timber, and a tornado with a water-spout played parts—a nightmare of nocturnal navigation !

At Nsake we intended to land the troops and reorganise for a second attempt, but on 10th October it was reported by the native pilots that the final fall of the river had begun, making it urgently necessary to get the larger vessels into deeper water. So we continued our journey to Wuri Island, and here, whilst the disembarkation was about to commence, the General Commanding arrived and ordered the expedition to return to Duala, where preparations were at once made for a second attempt.

After some changes in the composition of the force—the 1st Nigerian Regiment, under Lieut. Col. Cockburn,

WEST AFRICAN REGIMENT CHECKED BY MACHINE-GUN FIRE AT EDGE OF SWAMP, JABASSI, 7.10.1915

and a composite Battalion under Lieut. Col. Rose, replacing the West African Regiment—the flotilla was able to leave Duala on 13th October, the level of the river not having fallen so rapidly as was anticipated, but the current was racing down very strongly, and it was not till after sundown that the expedition halted at Nsake, which was found to be deserted by the enemy.

On the early morning of the 14th the advance upon the town commenced, the general plan being slightly changed in the light of experience gained during the first attempt.

On this occasion the armed boats of the flotilla led by the *Dreadnought*, on which we established Headquarters, moved slowly up stream supporting the troops on both banks, the right bank detachment consisting of $3\frac{1}{2}$ companies of Infantry and a section of mountain guns under Lieut. Col. Cockburn, and the left $2\frac{1}{2}$ companies under Lieut. Col. Rose, to whom surf-boats were supplied to negotiate unfordable swamps intersecting the line of advance. The remainder of the troops were kept in

OUR TROOPS RESTING ON LIGHTERS IN WURI RIVER AFTER CAPTURE
OF JABASSI

reserve in the boats following the armed craft and in readiness to reinforce either bank. At about 12 noon the enemy was engaged on both sides, falling back slowly as we advanced. By 1 p.m. we were within half a mile of the main position when the troops came under fairly heavy fire ; the defence, however, gradually slackened, and by 3 p.m. the men of Colonel Cockburn's flank detachment which he had launched earlier in the day, were seen on the high ground above the town. A general forward move was then made and the position on both banks was occupied by 4 p.m.

Several Germans were captured and the enemy suffered considerable losses, retreating towards Nyamtam on the east and Njanga on the west. Our troops entrenched themselves in the captured positions on both sides of the river and the flotilla lay between them for the night. On the 15th we followed up the enemy, who after some desultory fighting in the forest finally withdrew.

I mentioned that we had established Headquarters on the *Dreadnought* during the advance up the river. A

" BRUIX " CROISEUR CUIRASSÉ, 4735 TONS, AT THE BASE, SUELLABA

fearsome experience, for every time the 6-inch gun was fired, not only were we thrown off our feet, but the old lighter seemed to split in two—also our poor heads. As one of the bluejackets remarked when I ventured to ask him if he thought the lighter would hold together :

" It's like this 'ere, sir—she's out of place on this 'ere himpoverished (improvised) platform." (" She " being the 6-inch gun.)

On 16th October the expedition having completed its mission, returned to Duala, leaving Colonel Cockburn with his Nigerian Battalion in occupation of Jabassi and district.

The failure to seize the place at the first attempt was due chiefly to lack of information as to the nature of the country and enemy's strength ; to the fierce heat of the sun in the Wuri valley, which exhausted Europeans and natives alike ; also, in some measure, to the expert handling of the enemy machine-guns which caused some wavering in the ranks of the West African Regiment, this being their first experience of modern methods of slaughter ! Still, the enemy was fairly shaken, thus paving the way for our success of the 14th. All things considered, our losses were slight. Captain Brand, Royal Fusiliers, a dear good fellow and an officer of great promise, was our first casualty ; he was killed leading his men through the swamps. We also lost three British N.C.O.'s killed, two officers wounded, including Lieutenant R. D. Bennett, Middlesex Regiment, and machine-gun officer of the W.A.R., who worked the guns valiantly until the teams were practically wiped out, when they bore him off the field. A few bluejackets and some forty native soldiers were killed and wounded. Had the enemy shown more enterprise, there would no doubt have been a different story to tell ; perhaps we were unduly favoured by the fortune of war. In any case, it was a sweltering business, and I think we were all glad to get out of that infernal valley.

While the Jabassi affair was in progress, preparations were being made at G.H.Q. to commence operations in other areas. On 7th October the *Bruix* sailed for Libreville (French Congo) with orders to join the French gunboat *Surprise*[1] and to return with her to Duala, reconnoitring on the way the southern coast as far as the entrance to the

[1] On 21st September, the *Surprise* had already taken part in operations conducted from Libreville against a German force entrenched at Coco Beach, Corisco Bay. These were successful, and two armed enemy steamers were sunk, an officer and two men of the *Surprise* being killed.

Nyong river. She was further ordered to attack and disperse as far as possible any enemy concentrations in those regions.

The *Ivy*, also, after investigating German settlements near Rio del Rey, on the Nigerian frontier, was sent to survey the mouth of the Sanaga river, arriving there on the 12th and being met by the *Bruix* and *Surprise*, who had bombarded several German posts in their progress along the coast, but without affecting a landing. The French ships returned to Duala, while the *Ivy*, after surveying the

FALLS OF THE SANAGA RIVER AT EDEA

Sanaga bar, proceeded to the mouth of the Nyong and carried out a similar examination.

The result of these surveys was to show that though the Germans had apparently not used the rivers to any extent, the bars were quite practicable for small steamers, and in view of this knowledge an elaborate scheme of operations against Edea was planned to take full advantage of the water communications and of our now considerable flotilla.[1]

[1] No less than twenty guns, from six-inchers to Maxims, from the *Cumberland* and *Challenger* were mounted in various small craft, and apart from landing parties 220 naval ratings were employed in the flotilla.

The main military force which was to be provided by the French was to consist of 240 Europeans, 800 Senegalese Tirailleurs, and 1000 carriers, with 4 mountain guns. A detachment of 150 men of the W.A.R. under Captain R. D. Keyworth was also attached to the expedition, which was commanded by Colonel Mayer, the Commandant of the French contingent. This expedition was to proceed in six transports to the mouth of the Nyong and thence in small craft to Dehane, about twenty-five miles from the sea, where the troops were to disembark and march upon Edea. It was not anticipated that the enemy would expect an attack from this direction, and it was hoped that activity on the Sanaga would tend to distract their attention.

The Sanaga detachment was to consist of 150 men of the W.A.R. conveyed in small vessels together with the river monitors, armed tugs, etc. The small vessels to proceed through the sinuous Kwa Kwa Creek to Lobetal, a fortified post at the junction of the river and creek from which it was intended to drive the enemy and then join up with the monitors and larger vessels which, under Commander L. W. Braithwaite, R.N., would enter the river from seaward. The united flotilla was then to advance up river on Edea, establishing communication *en route* with Colonel Mayer's Nyong force.

The only naval help which could be given to the French force advancing from Yapoma along the Midland railway was the mounting of a 12 pdr. gun on an armoured truck and the despatch of the *Challenger's* field gun, escorted by a small party of the W.A.R.

The various detachments set out from Duala towards their appointed objectives on the evening of 20th October. The six transports for the Nyong river in line ahead astern of the *Cumberland* and screened to seaward by the *Dwarf* and *Surprise* arrived off the bar at daylight on the 21st, where they found the *Ivy* and small craft awaiting them. There was a heavy swell running on the bar,

1. COLONEL A. H. W. HAYWOOD, D.S.O., AND OFFICERS 2ND NIGERIAN REGIMENT. A FINE FIGHTING UNIT

2. MOUNTAIN GUN, NIGERIAN ARTILLERY, IN ACTION

3. THE GUN AFTER FIRING

4. BUILDING A BLOCKHOUSE ON NORTHERN RAILWAY

which not only impeded the transhipment of the troops, but caused a most regrettable accident to a boat which capsized in the surf, resulting in the drowning of Captain Childs, R.N., the superintendent of the Nigerian Marine, Commander Gray, R.N.R., Naval Transport Officer, and Captain Franqueville, a Staff officer of the French Army, all valuable lives whose loss it was difficult to replace. Captain Cyril Fuller, S.N.O., who was also in this boat, was rescued in an exhausted condition. He was awarded the Royal Humane Society's silver medal for his gallant efforts to save his brother officers. In spite of all difficulties, however, the advance guard was transferred to the river boats and proceeded up stream, while next day (22nd) the main body crossed the bar in the smaller transports and Dehane was occupied in the evening.

Both portions of the Sanaga expedition had been delayed and were unable to effect a junction at Lobetal until the 24th. The Kwa Kwa Creek detachment met with opposition on the 21st, and had a few casualties, and having failed to reach Lobetal, returned to Duala, which appeared to be a great waste of time. Renewing the attempt next day, it was found the enemy had evacuated his positions and Lobetal was occupied on the 23rd.

The monitors and other vessels which had proceeded by sea had experienced great difficulty in crossing the bar on the 21st—only the *Iron Duke* succeeded in entering the river. Next day, however, the *Remus*, *Porpoise*, and *Trojan* were able to cross, but the tug towing the *Dreadnought* grounded and became a total wreck. The *Dreadnought*, drifting out to sea, was picked up by the *Dwarf* on her way back from Nyong and towed to Duala. The remainder of the flotilla advanced up river, joining the Kwa Kwa Creek contingent at Lobetal on the 24th. Next day the advance up the Sanaga commenced, troops being landed on both banks to avoid the possibility of ambuscades, but there was little scrapping. On 26th October it was reported that the French had occupied

Edea; the flotilla then went ahead and anchored off the town that night. At first our Allies were strongly opposed in their advance from Dehane, which they had left on the 23rd, but from subsequent reports it appears that the enemy, when they heard the bellowing of the naval guns on the Sanaga, became alarmed and evacuated Edea rather than expose their black troops to the ordeal of a bombardment.

The evacuation of the town enabled the French force which had fought its way from Yapoma slowly and with difficulty along the railway to join hands with Colonel Mayer on the 28th, and the operation was successfully concluded, thanks in great measure to wholehearted co-operation on the part of the Navy. The feat performed by Commander Braithwaite in navigating the armed flotilla across the treacherous bar and through the narrow and tortuous channels of the Sanaga, won golden opinions from the landsmen.

GOVERNMENT HOUSE, BUEA

Whilst the movements ending in the capture of Jabassi and Edea were being pressed forward, Lieut. Col. A. H. W. Haywood, with the 2nd Nigerian Regiment, which had landed at Bonaberi after the fall of Duala, had so successfully fought his way and gained so much ground on the line of the Northern railway—having captured Susa— that General Dobell was able to turn his attention to the Cameroon mountain from which he determined to clear

the enemy, occupy Victoria and the coast-line to the Nigerian frontier and the hill-station of Buea with its military cantonment, Soppo. There was to be a naval demonstration at Victoria and other settlements along the coast, while converging columns of troops were to move on Buea ; Colonel Haywood continuing his advance up the Northern railway with Majuka as his next objective.

As O.C. British contingent it fell to my lot to conduct the operation and on 11th November two columns were formed, one at Duala (the Tiko column), the other at Mbonjo (based on Susa on the Northern railway). On the same day a detachment of Marines under Captain Hall, R.M.L.I., was despatched by sea to Victoria. The strength and composition of each column was as follows :—

Tiko Column : Commanding Lieut. Col. J. B. Cockburn, two 12 pdr. naval guns with detachments, No. 1 Battery Nigerian Artillery, 1st Battalion Nigeria Regiment, ½ company Pioneers, 1 company French Senegalese, Field Cable detachment, and 1000 carriers.

Mbonjo Column : Commanding Lieut. Col. R. A. de B. Rose, 1 Section Gold Coast Artillery, a composite Battalion Native troops, ½ company Pioneers, Field Cable detachment, and 600 carriers.

H.Q. British contingent accompanied the main (Tiko) column, which, embarking at Duala on the morning of 12th November in a flotilla of light draught vessels, arrived off Mbala in the Bimbia river at sundown and anchored for the night. At dawn on the 13th it moved up stream to Keka Haven pier, where the debarkation was completed by midday and the column bivouacked at Tiko with a covering detachment on the line Buta-Likombe. Early on the 14th the column, protected by flank companies, moved up the mountain towards its objective—Buea. At 10 a.m. the advance guard were driving in enemy scouts to the south of Dibamba heights on which the enemy had taken up an entrenched position, which was attacked by Colonel Cockburn's Nigerian Battalion, supported by the mountain guns. His men, sweeping over the heights in fine style, drove the enemy in all directions. Many of them in their hasty retreat shed boots and equipment, the more easily to avoid Nigerian bayonet-pricks.

Having cleared the position and the woods to front and

RUSTIC BRIDGE OVER MUNGO RIVER IN FOREST

flanks, the column pushed forward to Bole Fambe, and as the troops and carriers were showing signs of fatigue after ten hours' trekking and scrapping up steep gradients and through most difficult country, we formed bivouac and made ourselves snug for the night.

On the morning of the 15th we advanced to Molyko, where we were met by an officers' patrol from Lieut. Col. Rose's column, which was reported to be near Ekona blocking the roads leading northwards. After a short halt we continued our march on Buea, and on the way were met by a *parlementaire* surrendering the town, which we entered at noon, when the German District Commissioner handed us the keys of Government House, over which the Union Jack and Tricolour were duly displayed, the Allied guards presenting arms, the salute sounded by the Senegalese trumpeters reverberating round the mountain proclaiming victory to the scattered troops. Thus the town of Buea, with little bloodshed, passed into our hands. The units were at once allotted their billets and outposts, the British occupying Buea and the surrounding spurs of the mountain ; the French detachment, the military lines at Soppo.

Government House was an imposing structure of stone set in a garden of tropical luxuriance, and made a comfortable and convenient temporary Headquarters in a delightfully cool climate at an elevation of about 4500 feet, a contrast to the super-Turkish bath atmosphere of the Wuri valley. The building faced west, overlooking the Atlantic, and watching from the verandah the wonderful golden sunsets—a feature of the waning rainy season—with their ever-changing glories of colour and cloud, one was reminded of those beautiful lines from Moore's melodies :

> " And as I watch the line of light, that plays
>   Along the smooth wave tow'rd the burning west,
>   I long to tread that golden path of rays,
>   And think 'twould lead to some bright isle of rest."

In Government House were found some fine trophies of the chase, amongst them a magnificent pair of elephant tusks, probably the largest in Africa at that time, also two record giant eland horns (*orcas canna*), which now adorn the walls of the reading-room of the Junior Army and Navy Club.

Lieut. Col. Rose's column, which had concentrated at Mbonjo, on the Mungo river, commenced operations according to plan on 12th November, moving up the river banks to Mpundu and thence to Ekona and Lisoka, and after some Bush fighting marched into Buea on the 16th, having most successfully co-operated with the main (Tiko) column by blocking the enemy's line of retreat, capturing several prisoners, European and native, on the mountain-side and thoroughly clearing the country to the north and east. But though Colonel Rose successfully overcame all resistance offered by the Germans, some of his men were completely put out of action by a different kind of enemy, to wit, the wily elephant.

Courtesy of The Sphere.

ANOTHER ENEMY

There are regions to the north and east of the Cameroon mountain which at one time were actually dominated by these pachyderms—tracts of virgin forest country in which they were so numerous and hostile to human invasion that they have been known to attack individuals or even small parties of natives when making their way through the forest, in which there are many deep, sunken tracks leading from the low-lying country through the vales of the Mungo into the highlands, worn through countless ages by their mighty pads. It was through a portion of this old " Tuskers' domain " that Colonel Rose's column had to force its way, and the following account of the experiences of one of his junior officers on patrol duty is interesting. He writes :

"We had rather a trying time. Our Company Commander went out with myself and another subaltern and about forty men. We crossed the Mungo river in canoes and then did a long and very difficult march all through the night in dense forest country. How ever the guides managed it passed comprehension. About five in the morning, when it was just getting light, our advance party were on the point of stumbling on the German outpost when what should happen but an elephant suddenly walked in between and scattered both our opposing parties in all directions. I was in the rear of our little column and was left in bewilderment, all our carriers dropping their loads and everyone disappearing into the bush. After a few minutes we got our men together and our scouts went forward again to find the Germans had bolted from their outpost, but soon returned and opened fire on us."

On another occasion, during an attack on an enemy position, many of our men were put out of action by a cloud of wild bees, some of the poor fellows being so badly stung that they nearly died from pain and shock.

Whilst the land operations were being pressed forward, the Navy was playing its part on the coast-line. On 13th November a few shots were fired into Victoria to cover the landing of the Marines. The light mountain railway connecting Victoria with Buea was soon repaired and a regular service started by the detachment of Royal Engineers under Lieutenant Kentish, R.E. At about the same time, the *Dwarf*, with a transport, had appeared off Bibundi (east of Victoria), where a demonstration of landing was made, the *Dwarf* remaining and burning searchlights during the night.

Our casualties during these mountain "drives" were trifling compared with those of the enemy, who lost several officers and native soldiers killed, wounded, and captured, and some escaped through the forest. We also collected and despatched to Duala about a hundred Government officials, settlers, missionaries, and traders, with many women and children—quite a respectable bag.

As a result of the movements described in this chapter, the neighbourhood of Duala and practically the whole coastal region of Cameroons were made secure and the enemy thrown back into the interior.

In all this preliminary amphibious phase, the Navy and

Courtesy of London Electrotype Agency.

BEES IN BATTLE   APES ON THE WAR PATH

Nigerian marine played a most important and conspicuous part—carrying out such diverse duties as surveying, blockade, mine-sweeping, and clearances; repairing, arming, and manning the flotilla, providing artillery and detachments of seamen and Marines to assist the land operations and many other services, thus giving the native troops a real good send-off on their future arduous tasks in the vast hinterlands.

On the military commander of Buea and Victoria district, who was taken prisoner, was found a letter from the officer commanding the German force which was

M

opposing Lieut. Col. Haywood's advance on the Northern railway. Some extracts are taken from this letter as indicating the mentality of some of the German Colonial military officers of those days and their attitude towards the civilian officials in the Colony. The writer dates his letter 24/10/14, from Camp Majuka, and the translation runs :

" Dear ——,

Have just an hour to spare to write you a letter. It was very near ' nearly ' with me personally at Susa, I came through, and am still able to conduct further operations. . . ." (Then comes a long-drawn-out appreciation of the military situation from the writer's point of view.) Then : " Here we are fighting amongst beasts, our soldiers as well as the British and the negro beasts of the country make use of the war to rob and maltreat. This war, called up by the British, not only destroys all European value here, but stirs up the whole infamous negro soul." . . . " For the working of our civil authorities I have nothing but contempt. I would like to survive the war in order to tear down the curtain without mercy. If we do not reorganise from top to bottom—if the councillors of the Colonial Office crowd are not thrown out—if the conceited and useless officialdom at the head of the Government in Buea is not played out—then I will turn away, considering myself too good for this Augean stable of most sorrowful, ethical, social, and conceitedly stupid selection of exalted wisdom. You can imagine how I like ' chewing up ' the Buea people. Please show these officials everywhere that they are now at last in the hands of an

A PROSPEROUS CHIEFTAIN
WITH RETAINERS

uncontrolled military dictator, and have nothing to think about except how they can fill their stomachs. I always jump on them properly. It is nice once in a way, to be a soldier, and to be on top. Here I recognise no civil authority, only martial law. Under the aristocratic rule of military absolutism, the best of a man does come out. Everyone, whether planter or merchant, petty official or engine-driver, or whatever they are, feels better than he ever did before. How is it going with the dynamite plans in Victoria and the other places—and with the sea mines ? "

A clear case of :

> " Man, proud man !
> Dressed in a little brief authority . . .
> Plays such fantastic tricks before high Heaven
> As make the angels weep."

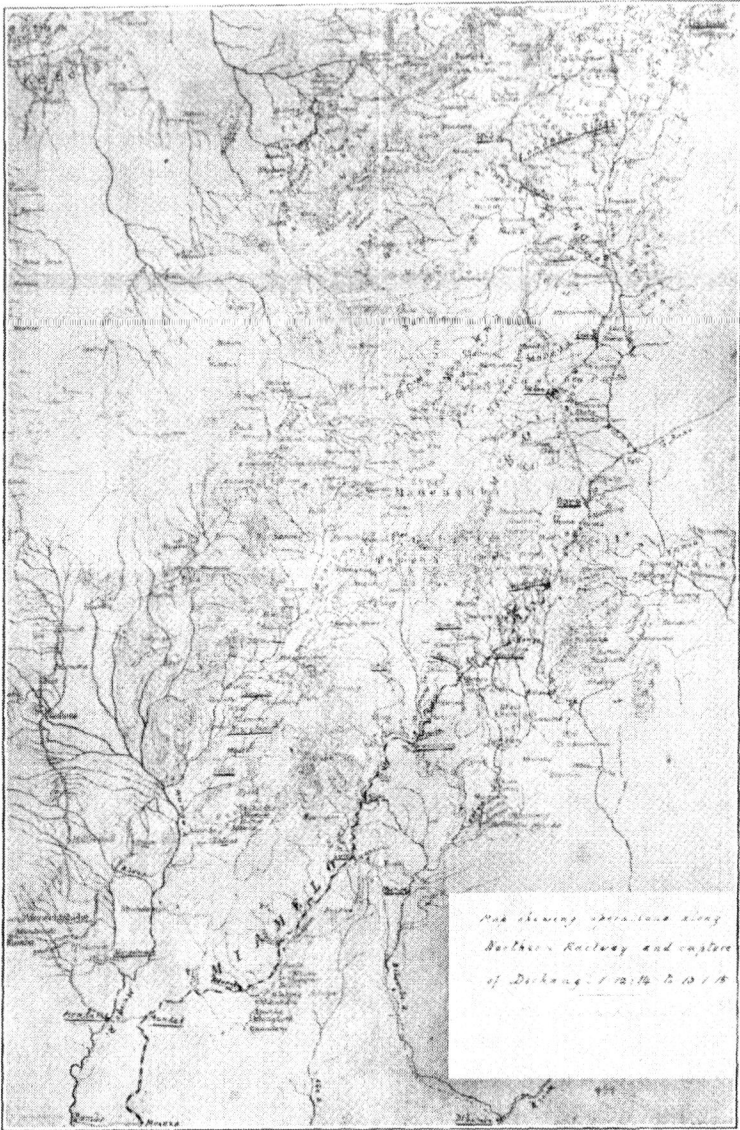

CAPTURED GERMAN MAP SHOWING ADVANCE OF BRITISH COLUMN
FROM MAJUKA ALONG NORTHERN RAILWAY TO DSCHANG

APPROXIMATE SCALE : 1″ = 20 MILES

CHAPTER IX

HAVING driven the Germans from the whole region of Cameroon mountain and firmly established ourselves in their " Summer capital," General Dobell, with the twofold object of striking an effective blow at the enemy and at the same time relieving the pressure on the southern Nigerian frontier, decided to clear the whole of the Northern railway and appointed me to command the expedition.

Accordingly, after settling preliminaries at Duala, I proceeded with my Staff on 1st December, 1914, to Majuka (kilo 60 on the Northern railway) which had recently been captured by Colonel Haywood's Nigerian Battalion. Here we found the main column with all ranks in good fighting trim and in readiness for the forward move.

The troops placed at my disposal for the operation were distributed as follows :—

At Majuka: Headquarters British contingent, $1\frac{1}{2}$ Battalions Nigeria Regiment, 1 Pioneer Company, 5 mountain guns, a detachment R.E. (Field Telegraph and Railway Sections), 1 12 pdr. naval gun with crew from the *Challenger* and Field Hospital. *At Mundame,* on the Mungo, west of the railway : a detachment of $\frac{1}{2}$ Battalion Nigeria Regiment and a mountain gun under Captain C. Gibb. *At Dibombe,* at the junction of the Wuri and Dibombe rivers—east of railway : 2 Companies West African Regiment under Major J. P. Law holding in check an enemy force in the Jabassi district.[1] *On the line of communication*—Bonaberi to Majuka : 3 companies West African Regiment under Major H. W. G. Meyer-Griffith. There were some 2000 transport carriers distributed amongst the units.

Briefly, this was our plan of action :

The main column to follow the railway line, while Captain Gibb's detachment moving up the valley of the Mungo river would protect our left flank and clear a large tract of country of small hostile bodies reported in that direction. Similarly, Major Law's detachment would move up the Dibombe river, thus securing our right flank.

As practically all engines and rolling stock were in the enemy's hands the main column had to march and carry its supplies by hand, until such time as the gods delivered unto us the spoils of war.

On 3rd December the main column advanced to Mundek against slight opposition. The right flank detachment working its way up the Dibombe through swamp and forest, surprised and defeated an enemy force at Njanga, capturing a machine-gun, a quantity of ammunition and stores. The left flank detachment occupied Mungo beach. On the 4th the main column seized Penja station ; the right detachment remaining at Njanga, the left reaching Gowe river ford—enemy snipers active throughout the day. On the 5th Lum station was occupied, the flank columns skilfully performing their rôle, the right moving up the Dibombe, the left reaching Nsake. Hearing loud explosions up the line during the night, a company with some R.E. under Captain J. W. Chamley was sent forward from Lum on the 5th to investigate and report upon the condition of the steel girder bridge which spanned the Dibombe river at Nlohe. The bridge,

---

[1] It should be noted that Jabassi, owing to the fall in the Wuri river, had become somewhat isolated, and that G.H.Q. had therefore withdrawn the garrison to Dibombe, where the waters were navigable.

1. DESTRUCTION OF NLOHE BRIDGE

2 & 3. AFTER HASTY REPAIR, OUR TROOPS CROSSING ON WABBLY
TRAINS, OFFICERS IN THE COAL-BOX !

completely destroyed, was lying in the rapids together
with some rolling stock. The company fell into an
ambush from which, after a combat in the forest lasting
several hours, Captain Chamley skilfully extricated his
men, falling back about a mile to the south of the bridge,
where, receiving a reinforcement from the main column,
a position was taken up astride the railway for the night
5th–6th December. We suffered some casualties in this
affair, including Lieutenant H. H. Schneider, R.E.,
killed, and Lieutenant C. Luxford, 1st Nigerias, wounded.
On the 6th the passage of the Dibombe was forced, the
R.E. and Captain Harvey Goodwin's pioneers building a
rough foot-bridge on the ruins of the destroyed railway
bridge of sufficient strength to pass troops, guns, and stores.
We also found intact, up stream near Nlohe village, one
of those cleverly constructed native twig suspension
bridges which served as an alternative crossing. Over
these two bridges troops were rapidly pushed, driving the
enemy north of Lala station, which was occupied by our
advance guard. Meanwhile the flank detachments had
worked their way forward, keeping abreast of the main
force, the left after a difficult crossing of the Mungo river,
occupied Ngushi, where some Germans and natives were
captured ; the right held the junction of the Dibombe
and Tinga rivers. The general movement northward
was continued on the 7th, and after a trying march under
a scorching sun during which we were subjected to
incessant sniping, we made Manengoteng station. During
the night our rest was again broken by a terrific explosion.
A truck containing a quantity of dynamite was set in
motion down line from the enemy camp, timed to explode
when it reached our bivouac. Fortunately the truck was
derailed and exploded at a point up the line where we
had taken the precaution to remove some rails.

As our line of communication was now stretching out
considerably, the advanced depôt was moved from
Majuka to Nlohe. On the 8th Manengole was captured,

DEFENCES ON LINE OF COMMUNICATION

whilst the left column moved eastward from Ngushi across the Kupe mountain to Edips, some four miles west of our position. The right column (Major Law's), having played its part with great exactness by keeping the Germans east of the Dibombe river, remained at Njanga. We met with a good deal of opposition during our advance on this day and inflicted some casualties, and the first consignment of rolling stock fell into our hands—four coaches, four trucks, and two good trollies. On the 9th the advance was continued through Manbellion where thirteen more carriages and trucks and several prisoners were taken. After clearing Manbellion we were warmly received in front and on both flanks, but managed to push north of Ndunge where a good entrenched bivouac was formed at the edge of the forest. Whilst digging in they sniped us heavily from the surrounding hills, but the country being now more open, the naval gun, to the delight of the bluejackets, was brought into action for the first time. This soon put the wind up the Germans and gave us a restful night. Had more casualties to-day, including Lieutenant L. C. Pateson, 1st Nigerias, severely wounded. The left flank column having reached Bengas, north-east of our position, a message was despatched to Captain Gibb requesting him to endeavour to co-operate closely with us on the morrow in the final move on rail-head, where it was hoped the enemy would make a stand. Captain Gibb was to move through Ekoahak and strike him in flank or get behind him whilst we engaged him on the railway, but owing to the difficult nature of the country we could not expect him to do more than move to the sound of the guns or rifle-fire.

On 10th December we entered a more open undulating country intersected by wooded valleys and ravines, and after a careful reconnaissance moved towards railhead. Our advance was strenuously opposed to kilometre 150, at which point a German officer with a small party under the white flag came forward and handed in a letter from the Commander of the enemy force intimating the surrender of the towns of Nkongsamba (railhead) and Bare, the latter six miles further north and the administrative centre of the district of that name. On receipt of this information we pushed on with all speed to grasp our prize, occupying railhead at noon and later in the day Captain Gibb marched in with the western column.

Courtesy of The Sphere.

COLOUR-SERGEANT POTTER WITH MACHINE-GUNNERS WEST AFRICAN REGIMENT IN ACTION AT NJANGA. THE TRIPOD WAS SMASHED, AND GUN WAS HELD IN POSITION BY ONE OF THE MEN

Outposts were thrown out on all sides, and the weary troops, after nine consecutive days of toil, enjoyed a brief, well-earned rest.

'Twas thus we slowly fought our way to railhead, the main column along the railway track between two walls of sombre forest in which aged and stately trees uprear themselves amidst weird and dark surroundings—where every hollow is a morass ; the undergrowth so thick tangled and knotted with rope-like creepers, struggling upwards to the sunlight; the ground so strewn with hidden fallen tree-trunks, that movement off the beaten track even for the strongest and most active is slow and irritating, headway only being possible with the constant plying of the axe. Intermittent rifle-fire, especially from "tree-snipers," and bursts of machine-gun fire added to our difficulties. When resting in the bivouacs it often occurred to me how the denizens of this region—the countless birds of brilliant plumage, the monkeys, the smaller reptiles dwelling on the great green roof of foliage that covers the forest, and those larger creatures inhabiting the depths beneath the canopy—must have been scared by the ceaseless din of musketry and machine-gun fire by day and the chattering of thousands of tongues in the bivouacs by night as the strife was carried through their domain.

The flank columns also had a rough passage, but surmounted all obstacles and carried out instructions almost to the letter, their splendid work being of material assistance to the general movement.

On the 11th Colonel Haywood with his Nigerian Battalion, a Section of Artillery and R.E. occupied Bare as our advanced base and suitable jumping-off place for another push into unknown spheres.

The spoils of war at railhead and Bare included five locomotives and tenders, fifty pieces of rolling stock—covered goods open trucks, 1st, 2nd, and 3rd compos and quantities of railway stores, tools and fuel, farming machines and implements, wagons and harness. In the railway store were two aeroplanes complete in every detail, quite a find in those early days of the War. Some welcome luxuries of the Fatherland in the tinned food and drink line fell into our hands or rather mouths—sweet champagne, beer, shinken, sauerkraut, leberwürst, and finally the live stock—a few mules and ponies, cattle, sheep, pigs and poultry, cats and dogs, in fact, most things that go to make up happy colonial homesteads, now ruthlessly broken up by *Die Heslige Englander*. Some prisoners were taken, and these with women, children, and a few missionaries were despatched to the base.

The attitude of the natives was friendly, and chiefs of local tribes with many followers trekked in from the

1. COLONEL COCKBURN'S BATTALION OF NIGERIANS MARCHING ON DSCHANG ROAD

2. A SHORT HALT

country-side bringing presents of food for the troops. One wizened white-haired old gentleman who came to pay his respects kept on muttering a curious jargon in melancholy tones for all the world like a Thibetan lama giving off prayers, the interpretation thereof being that he desired eternal friendship with the British and to offer his tribe *en masse* as labourers and carriers.

During our halt at railhead we received the news of Admiral Sturdee's victory off the Falklands. It was heartening to learn that the German squadron, save one ship, had gone to the bottom, and that the tragedy of Coronel had been redeemed. The tidings must have been particularly welcome to G.H.Q. and the Naval Staff at Duala, for their minds could no longer be disturbed by the unpleasant possibility of Von Spee crossing the southern Atlantic, cruising up the African coast and by the way destroying the whole of the Allied men-of-war and shipping sheltering in the Cameroon estuary.

Having rested the troops, reopened railway communication with the coast, replenished our magazine and driven the enemy from Melong (fourteen miles north of railhead), where Colonel Haywood had established a forward base and dumped therein a fortnight's supply, we were prepared to take the field again and to carry out the General's plan for the capture of the fort of Dschang, an important enemy post fifty-five miles north of railhead at the junction of several main roads leading E. to Fuman, N. to Bamenda, and W. through Tinto to Ikom, near the Nigerian border, where there was a British garrison with which we hoped to gain touch. So, after clearing our right towards Bana by driving an enemy detachment which had been menacing Bare across the Nkam river and readjusting our ever-lengthening L. of C., our diminishing force concentrated at Melong on Christmas Eve 1914.

Deducting L. of C. garrisons, casualties from action and sickness, we mustered about 1000 rifles with 6 mountain guns and the naval 12 pdr., by no means too strong a column for the work in hand; nevertheless all ranks were in good heart and getting into their stride in this new-fangled jumpy kind of ambuscade warfare, moreover we had unstinted support, abundant sympathy and encouragement from G.H.Q.

Two roads led northwards to Dschang, the right called by the Germans Government Road, up the valley of the

Nkam river through miles of elephant grass averaging about twelve feet in height ; the left through country

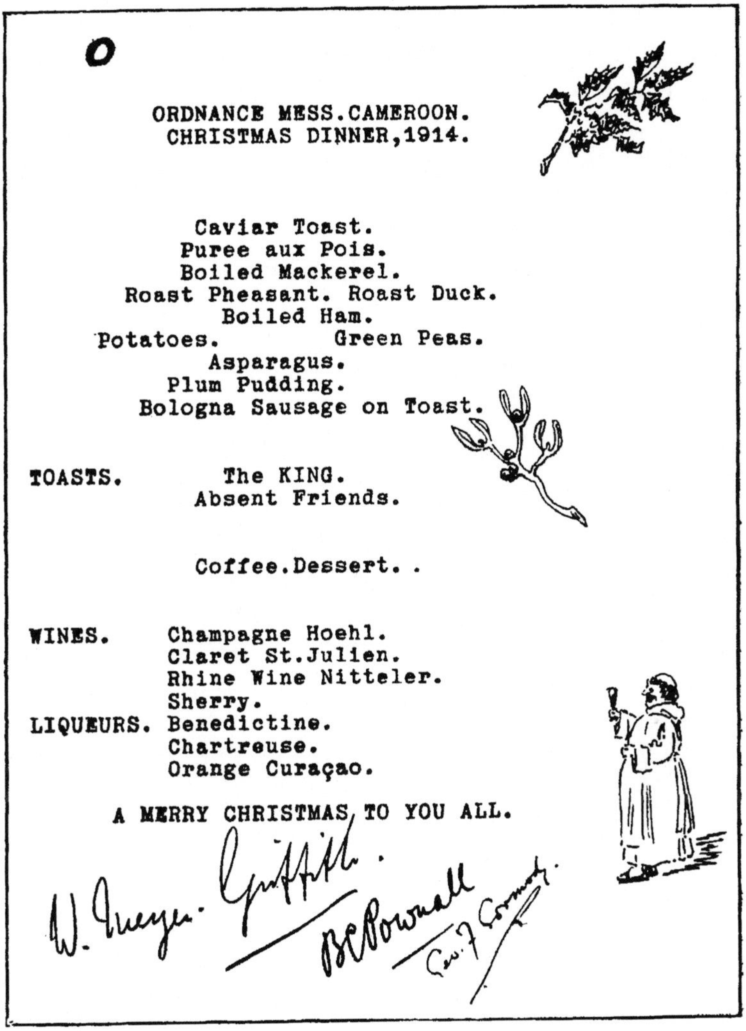

O

ORDNANCE MESS.CAMEROON.
CHRISTMAS DINNER,1914.

Caviar Toast.
Puree aux Pois.
Boiled Mackerel.
Roast Pheasant. Roast Duck.
Boiled Ham.
Potatoes.   Green Peas.
Asparagus.
Plum Pudding.
Bologna Sausage on Toast.

TOASTS.   The KING.
Absent Friends.

Coffee.Dessert. .

WINES.   Champagne Hoehl.
Claret St.Julien.
Rhine Wine Nitteler.
Sherry.
LIQUEURS. Benedictine.
Chartreuse.
Orange Curaçao.

A MERRY CHRISTMAS TO YOU ALL.

EXHIBIT MARKED O !

flanked by steep, rugged, thickly wooded heights, and twenty miles up this road on a spur of the Manenguba mountains was the fortified post of Mbo. As both roads were barred by the enemy we divided our force, detaching 2½ companies of the 2nd Nigeria Regiment and 2 mountain guns under Colonel Haywood up the left road, the main column with Headquarters moving by Government Road, and so on Christmas morn 1914 we ventured on our way.

A short distance along our road in a cleft stick was found a pencil note from the German Commander suggesting a Christmas truce ! but as we were not out for sighing and sobbing and wanted to get on with the business no answer was given, and after a fairly easy march during which patrols were constantly exchanging shots, a comfortable bivouac all amongst the elephant grass was found at Lelem. Here a quiet Christmas was spent, the " munching " and " bubbling " operations being postponed for a more appropriate setting. Talking of the festive season 1914. How were they spending it at the base (Duala) ? For reply *vide* exhibit marked O, and attached to the proceedings ! !

On the 26th the advance was continued to Mhu river, a tributary of the Nkam, the enemy falling back on Fongwang. Colonel Haywood was checked and became seriously engaged near Sanchu, and following a stubborn encounter in chamois-like surroundings the enemy withdrew to Mbo. Colonel Haywood's column suffered some losses, including Colour Sergeant J. Winter killed, less, however, than the enemy, who appeared to have been somewhat roughly handled.

After a restless night from mosquitoes, biting ants and enemy snipers who had found the range of our bivouac, the main column moved forward at daybreak on the 27th driving them from a succession of entrenchments over the Nkam river on the left bank of which a secure halting-place was discovered ; further casualties to-day, including Lieutenant O'Brien, 1st Nigerias, severely wounded whilst boldly leading the vanguard. The left column remained at Sanchu to enable Colonel Haywood to evacuate his wounded to Melong.

An officers' patrol under Lieutenants J. F. P. Butler and L. S. Biddulph, Gold Coast Regiment, sent out the previous day to round up a hostile detachment which had been harassing our right flank, rejoined us in the evening, having successfully carried out its mission. Lieutenant Butler swam the swift unfordable Nkam river under hostile fire to reconnoitre single-handed the enemy's dispositions and numbers, and for this and other remarkable acts of valour during the campaign this splendid young officer gained the V.C. He was killed later in the War, in East Africa, having also won the D.S.O.—one of the bravest of them all.

We had now left the elephant grass country and entered a forested mountain region in which after two days' fighting with an enemy whose presence was revealed only by intermittent bursts of machine-gun and rifle-fire, we outflanked and captured the Fondola ridge position.

NKAM RIVER FALLS, NEAR BARE

Here a halt was called to repair stretches of the mountain road destroyed by the Germans and the field telephone in the Nkam valley which had been carried away by a herd of elephants. The work was finished on New Year's Day 1915 when the hills at the juncture of the Mbo and Government Roads about seven miles south-west of Dschang were taken, and here Colonel Haywcod's column, after shifting the Germans from Mbo Fort, joined hands with us.

At daylight on 2nd January we advanced on Dschang, the transport column with a strong escort following at a safe distance. Movement was slow as the road ran through a narrow valley and it was necessary to clear the flanking heights. At midday a position within view of, and about

N

a mile from, the fort was reached. Here we halted to make final plans for carrying the place by assault.

During this lull in the strife we heard a great commotion in an adjacent wooded ravine from which there presently emerged a patrol of grinning Nigerians escorting a hefty German whom they had found hiding in the undergrowth. In a paroxysm of rage at being handled by black soldiers, he gesticulated wildly, using very bad language. He was led gently away by Lieutenant Jackson, R.E., and I was told later that he wanted to settle the fate of the campaign there and then, in single combat, on the ground on which we stood. Had any of us been so rash as to have accepted the challenge there can be no doubt that Germany would have won the War !

Supported by the mountain guns and the naval 12 pdr., the Infantry were making excellent progress when suddenly the German flag over the fort was hauled down and re-placed by the white. The garrison withdrew northwards, and as we moved towards our goal the troops were sub-jected to an intermittent musketry-fire from the surround-ing hills for quite an hour after the white flag had been displayed, which was not the first time during the campaign that the enemy had failed to follow the rules of war. It looked as though their black troops were getting a bit out of hand.

The fort, residency, settlement, and all neighbouring heights were in our possession before sundown and the Union Jack was hoisted on the fort flagstaff.

It seemed strange that the enemy would not stand and fight it out. Here was his opportunity, for we were some 150 miles from the coast with no chance of immediate help in the event of a reverse.

On 3rd January our patrols found enemy in some strength on the Bamenda road, but as our orders were to destroy the fort and then to evacuate and return to railhead, a column under Colonel Cockburn was sent out to engage him, whilst the remainder of the troops carried on the

work of demolition.   The fort was strongly built of brick
and cement with flanking towers and surrounded by a
wicked-looking cactus hedge.   It was no doubt originally
intended as a stronghold to resist raids from hostile local
tribes, but had apparently been recently strengthened in
view of a possible attack by our troops.   It would not have
withstood artillery fire for any length of time, especially

Courtesy of Illustrated London News.

THE NAVAL FIELD-GUN IN ACTION AT FONDOLA, 29.12.1914

from the naval gun, which probably accounted for the
precipitate evacuation.

Colonel Cockburn returned on the 5th having scattered
the enemy detachment estimated at 20 Europeans and
250 black troops, and as the demolitions were completed
on this day Colonel Haywood with his battalion and two
guns escorting prisoners, sick and wounded, marched
southward on the 6th, followed long before dawn on the
7th by the remainder of the force.   We slipped quietly
away, our guide the peerless light of a tropical moon
which " o'er the dark her silver mantle threw."   Silently

we toiled along until morn with all its grand features appeared, the sun topping the ridges, striking the trees with shafts of golden light, warming the air and letting loose African tongues.   Humming and buzzing voices mingled with peals of laughter echoed through the hills, and naturally the " palaver " was all about this sudden tail-turning to an enemy they had been chasing for the best part of three months.   The African mind could neither grasp nor appreciate such a situation, but this was a white man's quarrel and therefore Sergeant Major Sillah, Sergeant Bukare, Corporal Mamadu, and Private Kombo were satisfied !

It was unfortunate we could not hold on to Dschang, as a withdrawal gave a false impression to the natives and revived the enemy's spirits, but with a force much reduced in strength by casualties and sickness the General naturally did not feel justified in maintaining an isolated post nearly sixty miles from railhead, and joining hands with our own Nigerian troops at Ikom over the distant border was at that phase of the operations out of the question. So, unmolested, we retraced our footsteps southwards, concentrating at Bare and railhead on 10th January, 1915.

Thus ended the first venture into the hinterland which, if it did nothing else, gave an insight into the enemy's bush and mountain warfare tactics, duly noted for future guidance.   It was also a useful experience for the Supply and Medical Staff in handling the personnel and equipment of their respective departments.

Many of us at this stage were showing signs of wear and tear, especially the men, but their hearts were sound, and whilst praising the men we must put in a word for the transport carriers toiling ever with heavy loads, often under fire, suffering wounds and exhaustion, yet patient, uncomplaining and grateful even for an extra half ration, and above all for a few kindly and encouraging words—without the African carrier the operations could never have been undertaken.   Well ! here we were again, back

1. DSCHANG FORT

2. S.E. TOWER PROTECTED BY A STOUT CACTUS HEDGE

3. NAVAL FIELD-GUN AND BLUEJACKETS FROM H.M.S. "CHALLENGER" INSIDE THE CAPTURED FORT

in our old haunts after many days of sweat and toil, but then *absque sudore et labore nullum opus perfectum est.*

What was the next move ? It looked very much like a case of 2 Samuel, ch. x, v. 5—" Tarry at Jericho until your beards be grown." But we shall see !

On 5th January, as we were about to evacuate Dschang, the enemy made a determined effort to recapture Edea from the French. Colonel Zimmermann, the German Commander, had been preparing this blow for some time, but had been unable to keep his intentions altogether a secret from General Dobell, whose Intelligence Department was serving him well. Two attacks were made in rapid succession, the first against Kopongo, a post on the Midland railway, eight miles west of Edea, the second on Edea itself, a straggling township situated forty-five miles east of Duala on the left bank of the Sanaga river, on undulating ground in a clearing in the great forest, with fenced-in gardens and plantations and intersected by fairly good roads, while a labyrinth of forest pathways connected the various native villages and settlements on the outskirts. The Sanaga was spanned by a fine steel girder railway bridge which required careful guarding. It will thus be seen that Edea was by no means an easy place to defend.

The attack on Kopongo—delivered no doubt with the double object of first isolating the French in Edea, defeating them in detail and then investing Duala—failed.

That upon Edea was a more serious business, but so admirably had the French Commander (Colonel Mayer) planned his defences, so skilfully did the French officers handle their brave *tirailleurs,* and so accurate was their shooting that this attack also signally failed. At the close of the fight the Germans left on the field 23 Europeans dead and some 200 native soldiers killed and wounded. Machine-guns and a quantity of arms and ammunition were taken by the French whose casualties were trifling.

Following the Dschang adventure, the British troops

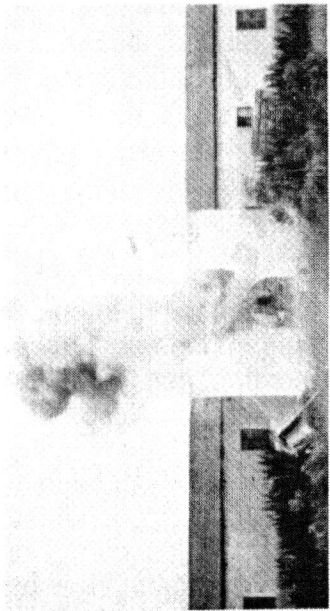

DESTRUCTION OF DSCHANG FORT BY PIONEERS OF GOLD COAST REGIMENT

had hardly settled down in their posts on the Northern railway when the enemy, as might have been anticipated, reappeared in the Bare district and commenced to harass our communications. By 1st February he had occupied a line extending from the Nkam river bridge on the Bana road through Harmann's farm on the Dschang road to the hamlets on the eastern slopes of Manenguba mountain around Mbureku.

Lieut. Col. Cockburn's Nigerian Battalion held Nkong-samba, whilst Bare was now garrisoned by Lieut. Col. G. P. Newstead's Sierra Leone Battalion of the " Waffs,"

Courtesy of London Electrotype Agency.

FRENCH OFFICERS LEADING THE TIRAILLEURS SENEGALAIS IN BAYONET CHARGE AT EDEA—1915

which had recently arrived with other troops as a welcome reinforcement to the Field Force.

The enemy became so aggressive that Cockburn deter-mined to take the offensive and fight him on his own ground at Mbureku, whilst Newstead engaged him north of Bare. Consequently Cockburn's column marched from Nkongsamba on the night of 2nd–3rd February hoping to surprise the enemy camp at dawn on the 3rd, but after a long and tiring night march, just as he was about to rest his men preparatory to the attack, his column was ambushed in the elephant grass. A confused and fierce night action ensued lasting from 3 a.m. until daylight in which charging, yelling, rattling of machine-guns and musketry, artillery fire at point-blank range, and stamped-ing of carriers played parts, the enemy being finally driven from the field.   This happy termination to Cockburn's

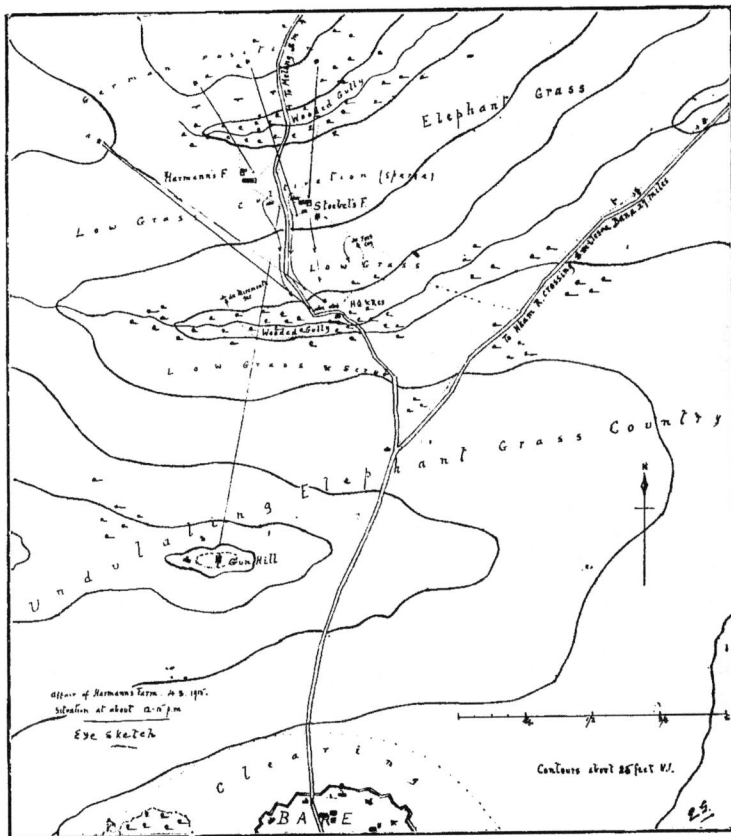

AFFAIR AT HARMANN'S FARM, 4.3.1915, 12-15 P.M.

fight was mainly due to that officer's bold and resolute leadership in a difficult and trying situation.   Newstead's column moved out from Bare on the morning of the same date as arranged and fought an indecisive action at Harmann's farm.   The tired troops then returned to their respective stations, whilst the Germans retired on Melong and the opposing sides lay low licking their wounds until the 19th, when they again met and fought on the slopes of Manenguba mountain and yet again on 27th February, neither side gaining any material advantage.

This series of minor engagements was hammered out on 3rd March, when by the General's orders we moved from railhead with a stronger force to attack the enemy at Melong. The main column, consisting of Sierra Leone

Courtesy of *Illustrated London News.*

AFFAIR AT HARMANN'S FARM.   CAUGHT UNDER GERMAN
MACHINE-GUN FIRE

troops (" Wars " and " Waffs "), advanced from Bare up the main north road, whilst the Gold Coast Regiment under Lieut. Col. H. de B. Rose moved on our left flank through Mbureku. The enemy was met in an entrenched position astride the road at Harmann's and Stoebel's farms, and after a severe encounter our troops under the strain of sustained and well-aimed fire from several concealed machine-guns, skilfully handled by Germans, gave way. The test was too tormenting, more than black

flesh and blood could bear, and in spite of the steadfast
example of their officers and British N.C.O.'s neither

ROUGH SKETCH OF BARE DISTRICT.   ENGAGEMENTS SHOWN BY
" CROSSED SWORDS "

" Momo " nor " Bokari " would on this occasion face any
more of the Maxim music.   Colonel Newstead, in a
supreme effort to sustain the fight, was mortally wounded :

my friend and Staff officer, Captain C. H. Dinnen, of whom I have already spoken, fell whilst doing his utmost to check the retrograde movement, and indeed many other officers of the Staff, the gunners and both the battalions engaged on this day displayed great devotion to their duty, conspicuous amongst them being Lieut. Col. A. J. Turner, D.S.O., General Staff, Lieut. Col. J. C. B. Statham, C.M.G., C.B.E., R.A.M.C., Lieut. Col. E. Vaughan, and Colour Sergeant R. Croft, W.A.R., also Captain Maclaverty, R.A., who was severely wounded. In fact, the cool and calm attitude of the officers generally enabled me to restore confidence in the troops and conduct an orderly retirement to Bare.[1] It was afterwards discovered—though too late—that the enemy's black troops were also shaken and that he had evacuated his position and retired north of Melong—such is the fortune of war.

During this series of actions our losses were somewhat severe, proportionately to the number of troops employed (8 British officers and N.C.O.'s and 140 native ranks), and little to show for them except that the Germans never again menaced our communications on this side, and barring active patrolling and a few minor bush combats the opposing forces remained in their respective spheres on either side of the Nkam river throughout the rainy season until the final Allied advance in October 1915.

[1] The Gold Coast Regiment did not take part in this engagement, as the retirement to Bare was ordered before it reached the scene of action.

CHAPTER X

EARLY in March 1915 the general situation was as follows :

GENERAL DOBELL'S ALLIED COMMAND

Headquarters at Duala. British troops holding the Northern railway and Bare. Dibombe, a fortified post on the Wuri river, thirty miles north of Duala. Victoria and the mountain railway to Soppo. Also Buea and practically the whole region of Cameroon mountain to the Nigerian frontier. French troops on the Midland railway as far as and including Edea, and a detachment in the coast town of Kribi.

GENERAL AYMERICH'S COMMAND

In August 1914 French forces from the Middle Congo invaded the Cameroons from the east and south-east. General Aymerich, the Commander, had formed two columns ; one under Colonel Hutin, which advanced from Bongo northwards up the Sanga river, the other under Colonel Morrison, westwards from Singa up the Lobaye ; that is to say through the territory Germany had acquired from France in 1911. These columns performed remarkably good work completely out of the limelight, the tide of conflict ebbing and flowing for long, weary months through the swamps and forests of that

THE PALM GROVE, DUALA

region, both sides suffering severely from casualties and sickness. In October 1914 the French had gained the line Carnot-Bania-Nola-Wesso, on the Sanga river ; here they were reinforced by a Belgian contingent of light artillery and 600 Tiraillers from the Congo, and continuing the westward movement, General Aymerich, by Christmas 1914, had captured Betare and Molundu, and in March 1915 his troops were approaching Dumie and Lomie.

There were also smaller French forces in motion whose activities had not hitherto had any effect on the general situation, but which now commenced to threaten the

BLOCKHOUSES AT BARE

Germans from the south-west. These, under Colonel Miquelard, cleared the enemy from German Muni and a column under Colonel le Meilleur was advancing northwards parallel with the eastern frontier of Spanish Guinea.

BRIGADIER GENERAL CUNLIFFE'S ALLIED COMMAND

This force comprised the troops of the West African Frontier Force holding the eastern frontier of Nigeria, with Headquarters at Yola, together with a French contingent under Colonel Brisset (a portion of General Largeau's command) from Fort Lamy in the Chad military territory which had invaded northern Cameroons, and after capturing Kusseri was about to join with us in the general offensive. Two smaller British columns were also included in General Cunliffe's command ; one based on Ibi guarding the frontier from Takum to Karbarbi in the Muri province, under Major G. D. Mann, R.A., the other at Ossidinge, on the Cross river, under Lieut. Col. G. T. Mair, D.S.O., R.A.

NAVAL ACTIVITY

During March and April the Allied naval forces systematically patrolled the Cameroon coast and adjoining trade routes. From midnight 23rd–24th April, in accordance with instructions from London and Paris, a formal blockade was declared, except for the entrance to the Cameroon river. This action was fully justified by evidence gained during the past months that German agents, with the assistance of German sympathisers in Fernando Po and Spanish Muni, had established between those places and the Cameroons a system of regular communication and convoys. Following the declaration, moreover, the Allies had the satisfaction of discovering from time to time from intercepted enemy letters and other sources, that cargoes seized had been intended for the German forces in Cameroons. All navigable waters of creeks and rivers were patrolled by the flotilla boats.

THE ENEMY

All these widely separated Allied columns were in contact with German forces whose strength and resources it was difficult accurately to estimate, so skilfully were they concealed and so resolutely were they handled in a country pre-eminently adapted to surprise attacks.

It will thus be noted that though we had gained a firm footing in the Colony, our efforts hitherto had of necessity been directed against purely local objectives ; each commander engaging the enemy where he found him, co-ordination of movement or intercommunication over so vast an area being unattainable. Operations had,

1 & 2. GERMAN-TRAINED NATIVE SOLDIERS

3. THE FINISHED ARTICLE !

however, at last reached a stage when it became possible to consider plans of closer co-operation.

Owing to the heavy task in which General Dobell was engaged at Duala, it was manifestly impossible at this stage for him to control movements from the Nigerian side ; it was consequently arranged that General Cunliffe should prosecute an active campaign from that quarter and that his first purpose should be the reduction of the fortress of Garua, whilst General Aymerich would, as far as distances and the nature of the country permitted, co-operate with General Dobell when the time arrived for

NAVAL 12 PDR. FROM " CHALLENGER "

a combined movement against Yaunde, now the seat of German Colonial administration and Military Head-quarters.

We will now follow Cunliffe's movements in the north :

After the reverses suffered by our troops along the Nigerian frontier in August and early September 1914, a policy of active defence had been pursued, and with the exception of a few enemy raids into the Muri province the frontier had been comparatively free from war's alarms.

Cunliffe, who in January 1915 had journeyed from Nigeria to Duala to confer with General Dobell as to

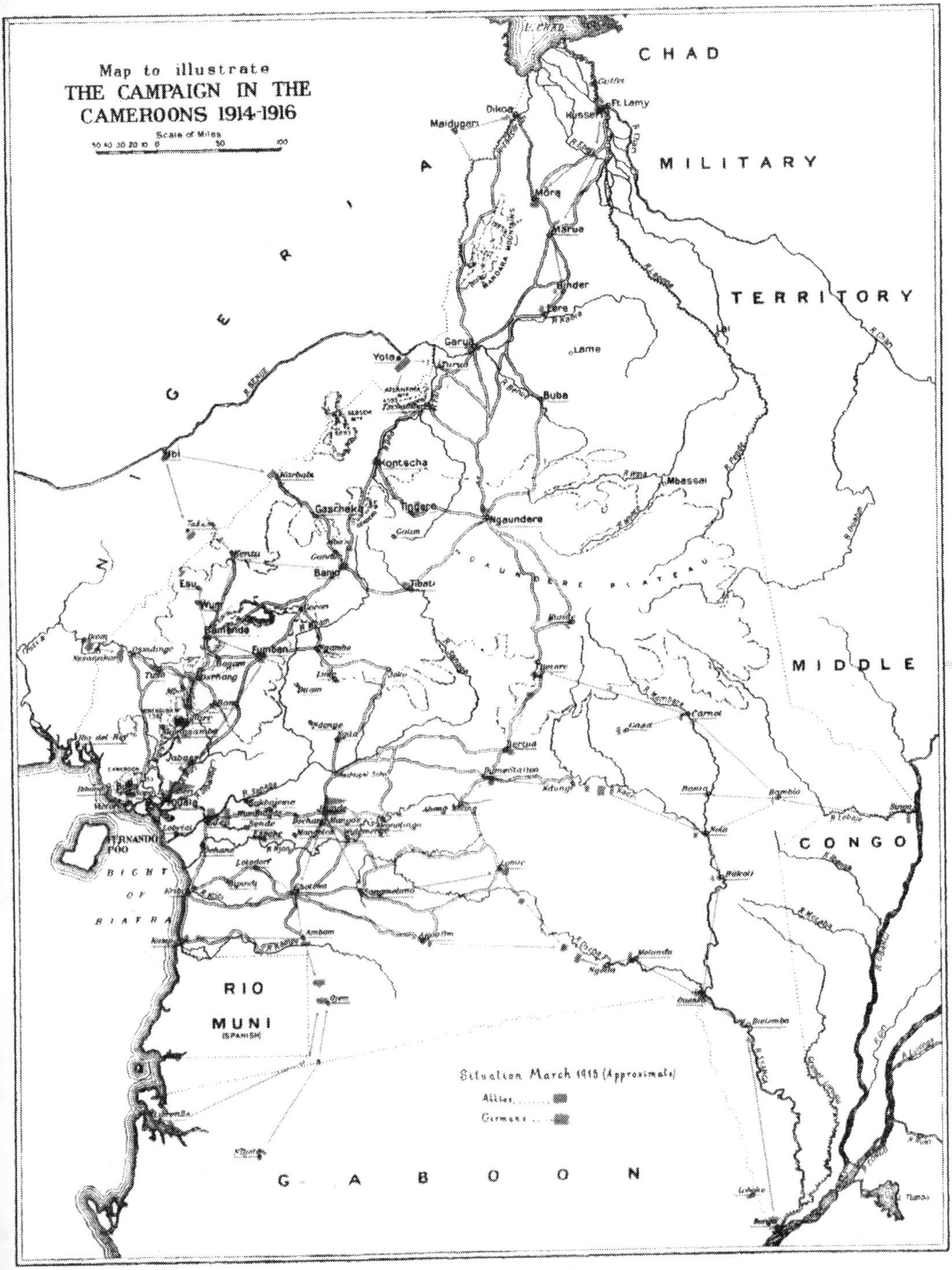

Map to illustrate
THE CAMPAIGN IN THE
CAMEROONS 1914-1916

Scale of Miles
50 40 30 20 10 0   50   100

CHAD

NIGERIA

MILITARY

TERRITORY

MIDDLE

CONGO

RIO
MUNI
(SPANISH)

BIGHT
OF
BIAFRA

FERNANDO
POO

GABOON

Situation March 1915 (Approximate)
Allies ....
Germans .....

future plans, returned to Lagos in February and reached
Yola on 15th March, where after discussing the situation
with the British Commander, Lieut. Col. W. I. Webb-
Bowen, Middlesex Regiment, and a French Staff officer,
he decided to concentrate as large a force as possible for
the reduction of Garua. To carry out his project he
ordered the withdrawal of three companies of infantry
from the Cross river and one from the Ibi column to Yola
and assembled under Colonel Brisset near Garua the
French troops which were scattered over a wide area.
This depletion of the middle and southern frontier

BENUE RIVER IN THE DRY SEASON. GARUA MOUNTAIN IN DISTANCE

columns entailed a risk of enemy raids to the Benue river,
the main communication, but risks had to be run, and as
a matter of fact an enemy column did cross the frontier,
and penetrating to the town of Mutum Bui near the river,
destroyed the residency, damaged a good deal of property,
and interrupted the telegraphic communication with the
coast from 12th–26th April.

As Garua was known to be strongly fortified and its
artillery to outrange that of the Allies, a 12 pdr., with
crew from the *Challenger* under Lieutenant Commander
L. H. K. Hamilton, R.N., had been despatched from
Lagos up the Niger and Benue rivers and reached Yola

on 12th March, while the French had arranged to send a 95 mm. by the same route.

On 18th April Cunliffe moved his headquarters to Bogole near Garua, and at once commenced to extend his troops with the object of preventing the enemy breaking away to the south and south-west. The strength of the investing force was : *British*, 8 companies of Infantry, 1 company Mounted Infantry, 3 guns (including the naval 12 pdr.), 9 machine-guns. *French*, 3 companies of Infantry, 1 squadron Cavalry, 2 guns, 2 mitrailleuses— by no means too large a force for the work in hand.

GARUA MOUNTAIN, THE GERMANS' GREAT NORTHERN STRONGHOLD, CAPTURED BY GENERAL CUNLIFFE'S TROOPS, 10.6.1915

During the night of 21st–22nd April a German column estimated at 10 Europeans, 100 mounted men, and 200 Infantry under Hauptmann von Crailsheim made a sortie from the fortress passing south to the westward of our investing troops. South of Tarna it was joined by a detachment which had moved north from Ngaundere. It was then completely lost sight of until one fine morning Cunliffe heard that von Crailsheim was attacking our frontier post of Gurin, forty miles south-west of Garua. The small garrison, though it lost its Commander, put up a splendid fight and finally beat off the Germans, who then

trekked southwards to Chamba, where they arrived on
1st May. From Chamba they moved across country and
evading the troops Cunliffe had despatched to intercept
them, made their way safely back to Garua, where they
arrived on 8th May.

Cunliffe having decided that the line of attack offering
the greatest prospect of success was from the north had,
by 25th May, concentrated the bulk of the British troops
at Jamboutu Manga, and the movement was so well
concealed that it was unknown to the enemy until the day
following its completion. From 26th to 28th May his men

A GATEWAY TO THE WALLED NATIVE TOWN OF GARUA

were subjected to a good deal of shelling from the forts,
but the arrival of the French 95 mm. gun on the latter
date finally gave him superiority of fire. By the 31st the
greater part of our force was entrenched within 5000 yards
of the outer works, then, sapping under cover of darkness,
the troops pushed steadily forward until 9th June, when
a line of trenches with a frontage of about 400 yards was
established within 1000 yards of the position, fed by good
communication trenches from the rear. The most difficult
question of all was the water supply, for the precious
liquid had to be carried to the advanced troops in pots
for more than two miles.

During the night of 9th–10th June two attempts were made by the enemy to break through our lines ; the first was nipped in the bud by the accurate fire of a company of Nigerians at Bilonde ; the second was disastrous to the Germans, for many of the men, discarding arms and equipment, tried to swim the flooded Benue. About fifty were able to stem the torrent and escaped, many were drowned—seventy bodies were recovered from the river—and the remainder made their way back to the fortress.

On the afternoon of 10th June whilst preparations were being made to carry the place by assault, the white flag was suddenly displayed. It appears that the native soldiery had got completely out of hand, the fire of our heavier guns having played such havoc that they could no longer endure the strain ; though it is but fair to say that having regard to the ordeal they were called upon to face, they stuck to their post with credit to themselves and their officers. At first the Commander offered to capitulate, but was informed by General Cunliffe that, failing unconditional surrender within two hours, hostilities would be reopened. At the last minute of the time allowance the garrison surrendered with 37 Europeans, 220 native ranks, 5 guns, 10 Maxims, together with a quantity of arms, ammunition, equipment, and stores.

Garua and its surroundings, naturally strong, had, by

A FRENCH COLUMN MARCHING FROM SO DIBANGA TO JOIN BRITISH AT WUM BIAGAS

every means which the defenders could devise, been transformed into what they believed to be an almost impregnable position, no less than 2000 native labourers having been employed under European supervision for five months on the defences. It was fortunate therefore that the place was surrendered before our troops were committed to an assault.

Cunliffe determined to follow up his success by seizing, if possible, Ngaundere, an important town where several roads meet, 140 miles due south of Garua, and also the northern fringe of the plateau of that name; for, if successful, he would frustrate an enemy concentration there and secure a line from which he could at a later stage advance southwards to co-operate against the main objective, Yaunde.

A COMPANY OF NIGERIANS CROSSING
MBILA RIVER BRIDGE

Accordingly, he directed Lieut. Col. Webb-Bowen's column southwards on Ngaundere, instructing Colonel Brisset, who now commanded at Garua, to furnish Webb-Bowen with reinforcements as required and, in order that he might be in direct telegraphic communication with Lagos and Duala, Cunliffe, on 15th June, moved his Headquarters back to Yola.

By 27th June his troops had occupied Kontscha and Tschamba, the enemy retiring towards Banyo, and on the 28th the German outposts holding the steep approaches to the northern edge of Ngaundere plateau were, in the midst of a blinding tornado, completely surprised and

routed by Webb-Bowen's advance guard under Captain
C. H. Fowle, Hampshire Regiment, who occupied the
town of Ngaundere that evening. The enemy counter-
attacked during the night, were repulsed and retired on
Tibati. Shortly afterwards Colonel Brisset with French
troops moved southwards from Garua into Ngaundere
and pushed reconnaissances towards Tibati and Kunde.

It was now that Cunliffe heard of the suspension of
Dobell's operations in the south, and whilst appreciating
the importance of seizing Banyo he was doubtful whether
under the changed circumstances he would be able to
maintain himself there, so wisely decided to content himself for the time being with the line Ngaundere-Kontscha-
Gashaka with a strong line of communication through the
Muri province to Ibi on the Benue. The fortress of Mora
still held out. This was the position in the northern
sphere at the beginning of July 1915.

We now leave Cunliffe in Yola with his successful
troops spread out in their bivouacs over some 200 miles
along the central plateau and turn again southwards to
Duala, where on 12th March a mission from French
Equatorial Africa, headed by M. Fourneau, Lieutenant
Governor of the Middle Congo, had arrived to invite
General Dobell to make an immediate advance on Yaunde
in conjunction with General Aymerich's force. Dobell,
while fully realising the political and strategical importance
of Yaunde, was not at the moment in favour of embarking
on such an operation. The heavy rains were setting in
and the troops at his disposal were insufficient to ensure
success in the absence of effective co-operation in the
immediate neighbourhood of the objective, which it was
unsafe to rely upon owing to the distances involved and
difficulties of communication. Nevertheless, in deference
to the Governor's appeal and in view of the advantages
to be gained by an early occupation of Yaunde, Dobell
finally waived objections and agreed to co-operate with
all his available resources.

The plan for the first stage was to force the passage of the Kele river, capture Ngwe and So Dibanga and then push eastwards and occupy the line Wum Biagas (on the Mbila river) –Eseka (railhead of Midland railway), and in order to protect our left flank during the movement it was necessary to send a small force northwards to Sakbajeme to deny the crossing of the Sanaga river at that place to the enemy.

Two columns were employed, the northern or Wum Biagas, consisting of Nigerian troops under Lieut. Col.

BIVOUAC IN FOREST CLEARING

Haywood, and the southern or Eseka, of French under Commandant Mechet. When these first objectives were gained, Mechet was to march northwards and join hands with Haywood at Wum Biagas ; the united force was then to continue operations under Colonel Mayer, Commander of the French contingent.

Both Ngwe and So Dibanga were obstinately defended, causing us a number of casualties ; the advance, however, from those places commenced as arranged on 1st May. Ndupe was captured on the 3rd and Wum Biagas on the 4th, but not without serious losses in European officers and native ranks. The enemy's position on the left bank of the Mbila river (a tributary of the Sanaga) was so strongly entrenched that it was not until after eighteen hours' hard fighting it was carried with unwavering perseverance by Haywood's Nigerians. The French move on Eseka also proved to be a difficult task, many railway bridges having been destroyed ; nevertheless, Colonel Metchet's Tirailleurs occupied the place on 11th May. He then marched northwards and joined hands with Haywood at Wum Biagas, when Colonel Mayer assumed command of the combined force.

General Dobell now learned that the French columns under General Aymerich had not yet reached their immediate objective— the line Dumie-Lome, 140 miles east of Yaunde—and that in consequence no date could be named for a west- ward move from that line. This was not a very soothing piece of intelli- gence for our G.O.C., but having fulfilled his engagement and com- mitted his troops he decided to press onward and eastward, and Colonel Mayer advanced from Wum Biagas on 25th May. His column, about two thousand strong with a host of carriers, soon found itself in the grip of the primeval forest through which the men had to hack their way when off the beaten track, often up to their waists in swamp and ever in the face of an enemy disputing every yard of ground in well-chosen and concealed positions, the deluge of rain swelling the sea of trouble. Under such conditions it became increasingly difficult to carry forward supplies sufficient to maintain the force.

MAJOR MEYER-GRIFFITH (KILLED IN ACTION, CAMEROONS, 28.5.1915)

By 5th June Colonel Mayer had made good only twelve miles from his starting-point ; the rate of progress being about one mile a day and his goal—Yaunde—still fifty miles distant. Battle casualties and sickness were fast thinning his ranks, freedom of movement on one narrow forest road was impossible, and the enemy who had received reinforcements began to harass his flank and attack his convoys. In fact, the situation was becoming so strained that Colonel Mayer gave it as his opinion that a further advance was impracticable. The G.O.C. at once notified the Governor General of French Equatorial Africa of the state of affairs, intimating at the same time that failing a forward move by General Aymerich's columns the enterprise would have to be temporarily

TEMPORARY BLOCKHOUSE IN THE FOREST

abandoned. On the 7th he was informed that there was no further news and thereupon ordered a retirement. A serious attack on a large food convoy hastened the backward movement, and during the 16th and 17th June our column was so hard pressed and roughly handled that a reinforcement of the last troops at the G.O.C.'s disposal, which had left Duala on the 15th, reached the column at a most opportune moment and practically saved the situation ; but it was not until 28th June that opposition finally ceased and the battered and exhausted troops came to rest in their soddened bivouacs on the line from which they had set out on 1st May. Our men and the French fought with great courage, the casualties reaching 25 per cent of the troops engaged, while dysentery and fevers still further weakened the ranks. The enemy too received severe blows and suffered heavy losses, but under good leadership fought with skill and determination, winning on point : *Alea belli incerta.* In the casualty list was the name of Major Meyer-Griffith, reserve of officers, commanding the line of communication, mortally wounded on 28th May, 1915, near Wum Biagas, when engaged in an effort to extricate a convoy of sick and wounded which had been ambushed in the forest. At the time he was leading a party of Tirailleurs Senegalais in a bayonet charge, and several of these brave fellows fell round him. They saved the convoy. Walter Meyer-Griffith, Croix de Guerre, was a gallant and gifted English gentleman of the best type. He was an enthusiastic soldier, too, held in high esteem by all who gained his friendship.

" L'homme loyal et généreux, l'ami sûr et fidèle, l'artiste aimant le noble et le beau, l'officier à l'esprit cultivé, qui a l'occasion devait être la bravoure personifiée, et il l'à d'ailleurs beaucoup trop prouvé près Wum Biagas, 28 mai, 1915.—Souvenir d'un officier français.

Whilst the fighting described in this chapter was in full swing, the Sierra Leone and Gold Coast troops holding the Northern railway enjoyed a period of comparative rest, the Germans since the early days of March having left them so severely alone that officers were able to indulge in various forms of sport—wild-fowl shooting, fishing, etc., whilst intercompany and regimental sports and competitions were organised for and much appreciated by the native soldiers. Moreover, a supply of vegetable seeds having arrived from England, those with a horticultural turn of mind enjoyed the time of their lives. There were vast clearings, followed by high fencings and then intensive sowings in the sheltered vales hard by the settlements, and with the coming of the rains a spirit of friendly horticultural rivalry hovered over the plantations. So fertile was the soil that dwarf beans soon grew to giants ; " runners " ran riot, climbing the trunks and festooning the branches of the great trees ; radishes assumed the proportions of mangel-wurzels and one turnip was a satisfying meal ; as to cabbages, a savoy of average size would almost feed a platoon. This is no " Traveller's tale " and a good advertisement for Sutton.

Though the district held a fair amount of big game of the water, reed, and bush buck species and some of the lesser antelopes, the undergrowth was so dense that shooting was a matter of great difficulty. Then there were large herds of elephants which at this season were roaming through the country and causing so much damage to the crops that local chiefs frequently begged us to hunt them down, and on one occasion my friend Lieutenant B. G. Atkin, of the Manchesters, and I answered the call. We

WELCOME RATIONS—BRACE OF WATERBUCK. DITTO REED-BUCK AND A BUSH-BUCK

trollied down the line twenty miles to Lala station and from there trekked through the forest in the direction in which the herd had last been seen, down the valley of the Dibombe. After many hours of gymnastics over fallen trees and broken branches which would have exhausted a troop of trained gorillas, we emerged on to a wide clearing, on the far side of which on gently rising ground we observed a small native village, for which we made a bee-line, hoping to obtain the latest news of the movements of the herd. To our amazement, however, as we approached our village it suddenly came to life, moved up the rise and disappeared into the forest.

" Great Cæsar's ghost, the——elephants ! " exclaimed

the agitated Atkin, and so it was, for the sudden change of light from the shade of the forest into the blazing sunlight had confused our vision and our ivory dream vanished with the herd. Disappointed, weary and footsore, we repaired to a native village hard by and there rested under the grateful shade of a magnificent mahogany, returning to the railway at sundown.

In the southern regions from July to October it was

A MAGNIFICENT MAHOGANY

impossible to engage in active operations on any scale owing to floods caused by heavy rains, consequently the General seized the opportunity to send as many British officers and non-commissioned officers as could be spared to England for a short period of change and rest, he likewise granted furlough in batches to the native ranks of the Gold Coast and Nigerian regiments to enable them to visit friends and relations in their own colonies.

As the rains in the north are very much lighter than in the south and therefore do not impede the movement of troops to the same extent, General Cunliffe determined, during the period of enforced inactivity in the south, to make an effort to capture the fortress of Mora which still held out, seeing that if successful his investing troops would be available for the final offensive, contemplated in the autumn. He left Yola on 9th August and arrived at Sava, four miles from Mora, on 23rd August. His force consisted of *British*, 1 company Mounted Infantry, 4 companies Infantry, 2 mountain guns ; *French*, 2 companies Infantry, 1 heavy gun. Examining the position,

GERMAN GARRISON, MORA (PRE-WAR)

he found that the slopes of the mountain, on the summit of which was Mora, rose precipitately to 1700 feet, were accessible in a few places only to men climbing with hands and feet and were strewn with huge boulders, which afforded excellent cover to the defenders, and all approaches were commanded by strongly built sangars, but in spite of the strength of the position he was resolved to capture it, if possible. The first and second attacks failed. The third gained a footing on the crest of the mountain where further progress was barred by a strong redoubt which a detachment of the 1st Nigerians tried to carry with the bayonet but were checked by heavy fire within a few yards of their goal. The men, however, stubbornly held on to the ground they had won for forty-eight hours without food or water, and it was not until every effort to supply them had failed that they were withdrawn. The attack lasted for eight days—1st–8th September—the German Commander of the fortress paying tribute to the bravery of the assaulting troops. The casualties included Captain R. N. Pike of the Nigerian

MORA MOUNTAIN

Political Service, whom Cunliffe describes as an officer of great courage and fearless leadership who had already distinguished himself on many occasions.[1]

It was now realised that to take Mora, a further supply of artillery ammunition would have to be brought up, but as Cunliffe's services were urgently required for the final sweep southwards, he was constrained to abandon the Mora undertaking, so leaving behind an Allied detach-

[1] The British losses during this operation were thirty-eight, including Captain Pike and sixteen natives killed, and Captain A. Gardner and Lieut. A. J. L. Cary wounded.

ment equal in strength to the original investing force, viz. 1 company Mounted Infantry and 3 companies Infantry, he marched southwards with the remainder on 17th September and arrived again at Yola on the 26th of that month.

On 25th August, 1915, there was held at Duala a second conference, on this occasion between General Dobell, M. Merlin, the Governor General of French Equatoria, and General Aymerich, at which the plan for the final phase of the campaign was agreed to and which was eventually crowned with success. As General Cunliffe was busily engaged in the north he was unable to attend, but the details of the scheme were duly communicated to him and he was asked to bring as much pressure to bear as possible when the columns were set in motion. We shall see later how he rose to the occasion.

P

CHAPTER XI

BY the end of October 1915 the sands of German dominion in West Africa were rapidly running down—Togoland and South-West Africa had gone, whilst in the Cameroons the Allied net was by slow degrees encircling enemy forces remaining in the field. The heavy rains in the coast region were subsiding, sickness was declining, officers and men were returning from recuperative leave, and furlough and considerable reinforcements of troops and transport carriers, both British and French, had so augmented General Dobell's command that preparations were sufficiently far advanced for a final effort by the Allied Commanders, whose columns were now disposed in varying strengths in the circumference of a rough circle, with Yaunde, the objective, as its centre, and where an early surrender of the German Colonial Government and forces was confidently anticipated.

In August General Dobell had asked Nigeria for another battalion of Nigerian troops, but these could not be spared from General Cunliffe's command. Some reinforcements had, however, been provided from other places, including the 5th Indian Light Infantry from India, half a company of Infantry from the Gambia, 2 companies of the West India Regiment and a detachment of Royal Engineers from Sierra Leone, and wastage drafts from all Colonies. Extra carriers had also been sent, the Governors of each Colony undertaking to maintain the necessary strength. From England had come a 4·5-inch howitzer with a British gun team, a wireless detachment, a Postal Section R.E. and a M.T. Company A.S.C. with armoured car, 25 Ford vans, and 6 ambulances. The French reinforcements included a Senegalese battalion and a number of French officers and drafts for Colonel Mayer's old units, and finally 2 com-

BRITISH OFFICERS AND NATIVE TROOPS FIGHTING A FIERCE BUSH FIRE

panies of Senegalese had arrived at Campo from Dakar on 27th October for Colonel le Meilleur's force.

Following a series of minor operations and engagements, during which positions were consolidated and road and railway communication greatly improved, our several groups of converging columns at the end of October 1915 were distributed as follows :

1. GENERAL DOBELL'S MAIN FORCE BASED ON DUALA

(a) A British column—Commander, Colonel Gorges.

Concentrating about Wum Biagas from which place the Germans had been driven on 9th October, after a severe engagement, by a force under Lieut. Col. Haywood's command.

(b) A French column—Commander, Colonel Mayer, which after stubborn fighting had captured Sende on 25th October and Eseka (where it was now concentrated) on the 30th.

(c) A British column (light)—Commander, Lieut. Col. Cotton. This column had marched from Bare, beyond the Northern railway, on 12th October and was fighting its way through the mountainous country about Mbo, towards Dschang, with the object of co-operating with Major Crookenden's detachment of General Cunliffe's command which was moving eastwards from Ossidinge towards Bamenda against strong opposition.

There were in addition Line of Communication troops on the Northern and Midland railways and a detachment observing the Jabassi district.

2. BRIGADIER GENERAL CUNLIFFE'S FORCE
BASED ON NIGERIA

Apart from a combined British and French detachment which was investing Mora, General Cunliffe's force early in October was disposed as follows :

(a) *Yolo*—His Headquarters—

> 3 mountain guns.
> 1 section Mounted Infantry.
> 3 companies Nigerian Infantry.

(b) *Takum–Karbabi–Geschaka*—

> $3\frac{1}{2}$ companies Nigerian Infantry—
> Major Mann.

(c) *Kontcha–Garua*—

> 2 companies Nigerian Infantry—
> Major Porter.

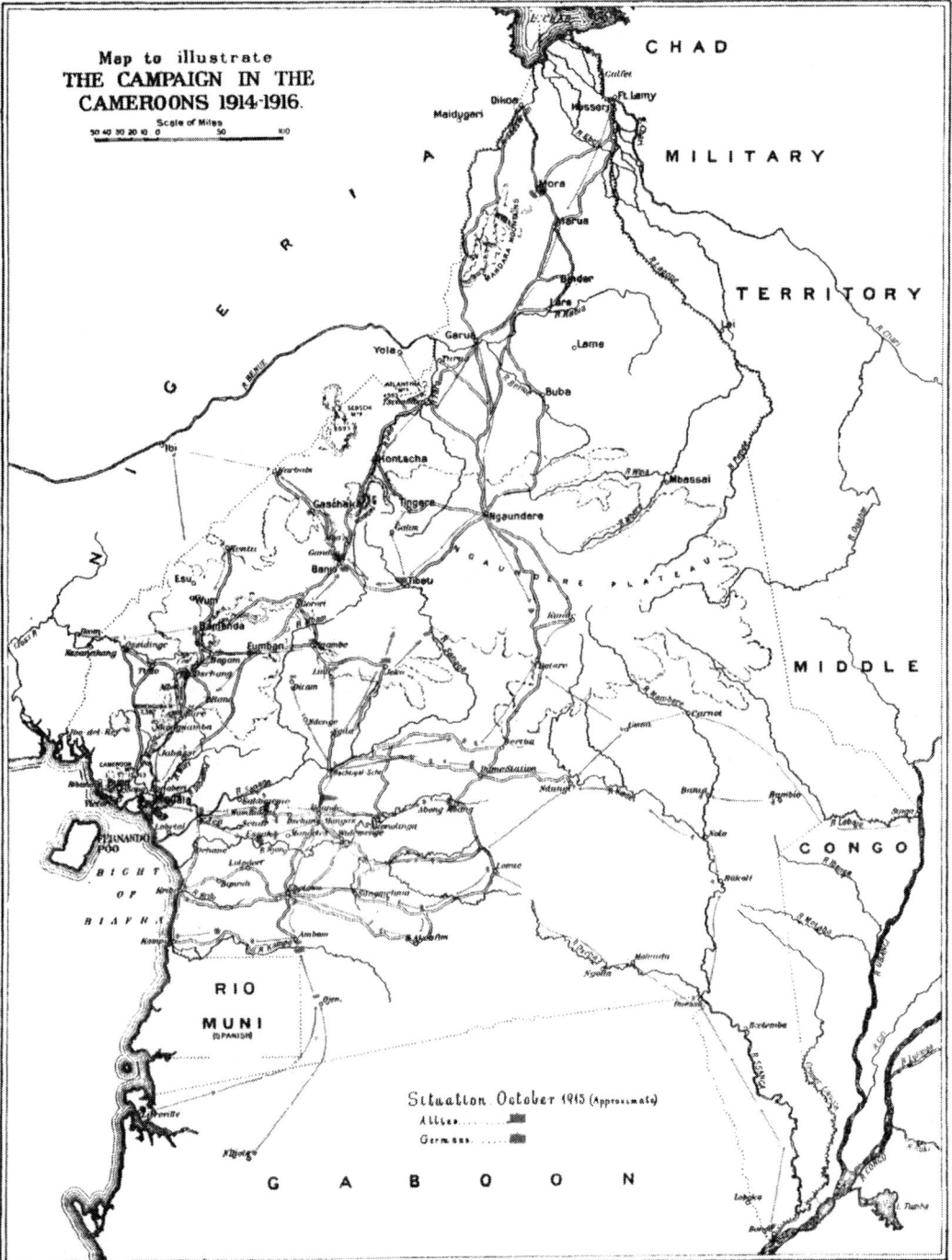

Map to illustrate
THE CAMPAIGN IN THE
CAMEROONS 1914-1916.

Scale of Miles

CHAD

MILITARY

TERRITORY

MIDDLE

CONGO

NIGERIA

GABOON

RIO
MUNI
(SPANISH)

BIGHT
OF
BIAFRA

FERNANDO
POO

Situation October 1915 (Approximate)
Allies..........
Germans.......

(*d*) Under Colonel Brisset's command—

    Tingere—2 companies Nigerian Infantry—Lieut. Col. Webb-Bowen.

    Ngaundere—1 squadron French Cavalry ⎱
             2 companies French Infantry ⎰ Col. Brisset.
             4 guns

With a third company about sixty miles south-east,

OUR PATROLS MOVING THROUGH THE FOREST

keeping in touch with Colonel Morrison's column moving on Kunde.

(*e*) *Ossidinge*—

        2 mountain guns ⎱
        4 companies Infantry ⎰ Major Crookenden.

Hoping to menace the enemy simultaneously from all sides, Cunliffe decided to move these columns against Bamenda–Banyo–Tibati. He ordered Crookenden from Ossidinge to Bamenda to co-operate with Colonel Cotton's column now moving on Dschang. His own and Major Mann's column were to converge on Banyo, while Colonel Brisset's troops from Tingere and Ngaundere were to seize Tibati. He moved his Headquarters from Yola to Kontscha on the 9th and on the 14th continued the movement on Banyo. At the end of the month his force was disposed as follows : Crookenden at Bamenda—Headquarters and main force Banyo—Colonel Brisset's columns approaching Tibati.

3. General Aymerich's Eastern Force

French troops with the Belgian contingent which, as we know, had been advancing steadily by river and road with varying fortunes from the Middle Congo, were now moving towards Yaunde from about the line Bertua–Dumie–Lome–Akoafim. The other French columns from Gabon, which under Colonel Miquelard had cleared German Muni, were marching northwards parallel with the eastern frontier of Spanish Guinea. Colonel le Meilleur's column had captured Oyem and Bitam (the latter by assault) and was now facing the enemy at Ambam, and the detachment of Senegalese under Captain Blum which had disembarked at Campo on 27th October was advancing along the Campo river to co-operate with Colonel le Meilleur, the intention being to prevent, if possible, the Germans escaping into the neutral territory.

Naval Operations

During September and October the Allied naval forces successfully maintained the blockade of the coast, frustrating attempts by natives to smuggle supplies to the enemy up the numerous rivers and creeks.

The Enemy's Forces

It was very difficult at this stage of the campaign to form a correct estimate of the actual strengths of the German forces still in the field. The casualties they had sustained from battle, sickness, prisoners of war and desertions since the commencement of operations—casualties which could not be replaced—must have been heavy, therefore a rough calculation had to be made. So successfully were their troops concealed that we shall never really know their actual strength until they produce their own history of this campaign. There were perhaps 1600 to 1700 holding Banyo–Tibati–Fumban and outposts on the central plateau—1800 south of the Sanaga river facing General Dobell's force, 1200 opposing General Aymerich and possibly another 800 south of Yaunde

GERMAN GOVERNOR AND STAFF IN THE BUSH

confronting the French columns moving towards Ebolowa —giving a total of about 5700 effectives, exclusive of the garrison of Mora. We shall now follow the movements of these Allied forces, which were actively in motion in November 1915 for the final phase of the campaign.

First we shall deal with General Dobell's operations through the forest towards Yaunde. The British column was at Wum Biagas, about sixty miles from Yaunde, with a covering detachment at Ngok and the French were still at Eseka (railhead), fifteen miles to the south of us.

The British column consisted of 2 battalions of the Nigeria Regiment, the Gold Coast Regiment, the Sierra Leone Battalion, the Gambia Company, and 2 companies of the West India Regiment, 6 mountain guns, detachment Royal Engineers and wireless sections, together with some 3000 transport carriers, an armoured car, and a few light Ford vans and ambulances. We were also saddled with the 4·5-inch field howitzer recently arrived from England with a British gun team. " Henry," as the gun was named, caused us no little anxiety, requiring as he did a host of carriers to haul him over the rough road and steep hills, and a permanent escort to guard him night and day, and though in that vast primeval forest he rarely, if ever, found a target, he was none the less cherished and admired by our own black soldiers, who, so long as they knew that " Henry " was in the bivouac, slept peacefully.

My Staff officers for this final push were the late Major H. Gwynne-Howell, D.S.O., Royal Artillery, General Staff, most capable and fearless and a first-class intelligence officer, and Major C. R. U. Savile, D.S.O., C.B.E., Royal Fusiliers (now Colonel General Staff). Jack Savile had been my Staff Captain from the commencement of the campaign. A fine officer, full of energy and military knowledge, with all manner of duties to perform, he yet found the time to be our Headquarters chef, and in that capacity kept the stock-pot full and simmering in all weathers and under all conditions. He had tact also, which in a country and climate where tempers varied as the ever-changing lights, was a priceless possession, and Jack Savile's tact was of the genuine type, not so commonly met with in the old army, and not to be confused with the habit of mind which not infrequently led an officer to take the least line of resistance for fear of injuring old Algy's interests or hurting dear Launcelot's feelings. That kind of tact is not to be commended, for it is liable to produce —as indeed it sometimes did—a regimental dry-rot.

Then there was Captain (now Lieut. Col.) B. G. Atkin, D.S.O., M.C., of my own regiment, whose personal friendship and kindly actions I so greatly valued during difficult days, and last, but by no means least, good old

ROUGH SKETCH MAP (EDEA-YAUNDE)

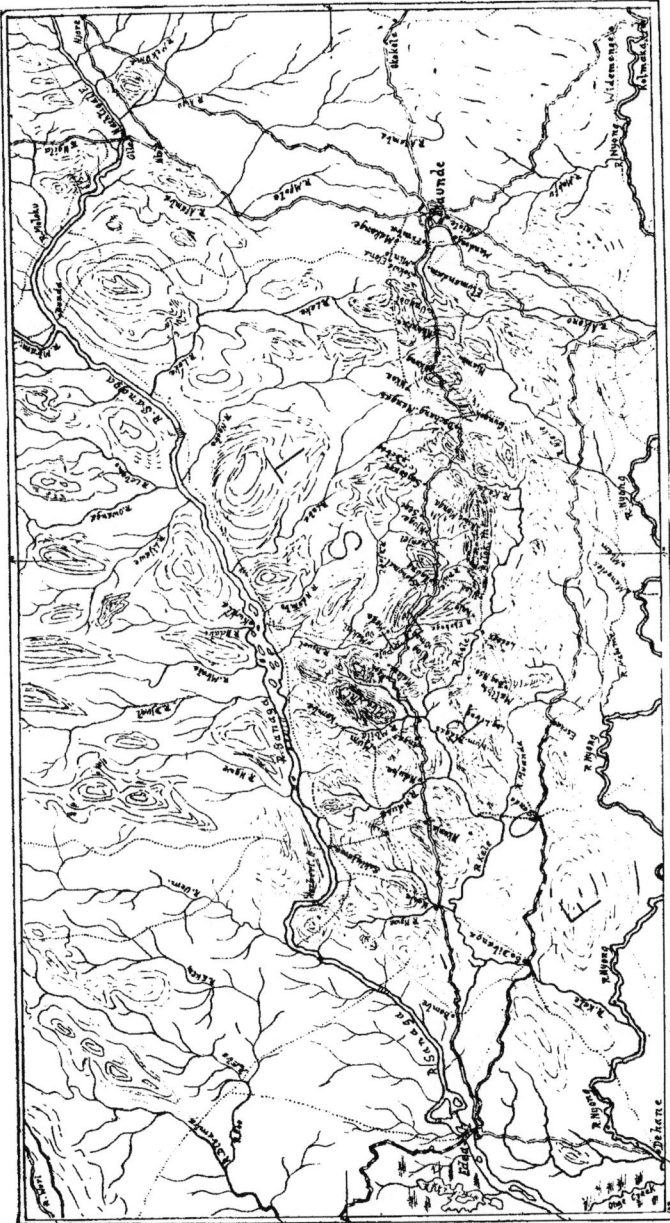

Rough sketch of country between EDEA and YAUNDE

Quartermaster Sergeant S. J. Cole—now a Brevet Major, O.B.E., and Staff officer to the Inspector General of the Royal W.A.F.F.—I hope his eye may some day catch these few words so that he may know his good work is still remembered. And now to return to the beaten track !

On 23rd November the G.O.C. ordered both columns forward. Dschang-Mangas, distant forty miles, was selected as the British first objective, while the French were to make good the nearest point on the Yaunde-Kribi road.

Our method of advance was to move a strong column along the forest road with two flank detachments, on as wide a front as the very difficult nature of the country permitted, every effort being made to keep the columns within supporting distance of each other. By this means we could keep our communications fairly safe and generally outmanœuvre the enemy from his chosen positions.

By 30th November, after seven days' strenuous scrapping —described by an officer as " forest fireworks "—we drove the Germans back nearly twelve miles on a frontage averaging from twelve to fifteen and occupied Ngung and roughly the line of the Puge river. Many strongly entrenched positions were turned and taken, some with the bayonet, and at Ngung itself, Captain L. S. Biddulph, the Gold Coast Regiment, led his company up a river bed through the densest forest, finally charging with the bayonet into the trenches from which the enemy fled in disorder. Off the road the troops had to work their way through very thick undergrowth covering precipitous hills, while in the valleys they had to wade through wide stretches of swamp, sometimes above their waists. Colonel Cockburn's battalion of Nigerians bore the brunt of the week's fighting on our right flank, forcing the passage of the Kele river near Lesogs, his losses in killed and wounded bearing witness to its conduct and work in the field and to Cockburn's fine leadership.[1] This kind of business made progress slow, and it was creditable to the men that after a few days' rest they were again eager to continue the struggle.

During our halt at Ngung we made a strong fortified post to contain a company of Infantry, magazine, store-houses, and hospital, and on 7th December, in our usual formation, we continued the pressure. It was slow and toilsome work dislodging the Germans from their well-sited and wonderfully constructed entrenchments along the Manjei river. However, by 10th December, Lieut. Col. Haywood's regiment, which had relieved Cockburn's on our right, had outflanked him in the Belok mountain, whilst Captain Butler, V.C., who led the left flank detachment of Gold Coast troops, surprised his camp at Sege, ten miles west of Dschang-

CAPTAIN B. G. ATKIN (NOW LIEUT. COLONEL, D.S.O., M.C.), THE MANCHESTER REGIMENT

Mangas, causing his soldiers to break and scatter in all directions, and capturing machine-gun, rifles, quantities of ammunition, stores and food, also documents containing useful information.

---

[1] The losses in this combat were 3 British officers and 19 natives killed or died of wounds, and 4 British officers and N.C.O.'s and 76 natives wounded.

Following this stroke, with Haywood forcing back his left, Butler still harassing his right and the main (centre) column pressing steadily forward, enemy resistance gradually weakened, and after driving him over the Kele river on the 15th, our first objective, Dschang-Mangas, was taken on 17th December. Here we halted again to rest, reorganise and build our last strong post before making a final dash into Yaunde, now twenty-five miles distant.

Dschang-Mangas lay on the eastern edge of the grim, twilight forest region in which we had experienced a good

THE SWAMP " ROAD "

deal of blind fighting which imposed a continuous strain on nerves now pretty well shaken by the climate, and perhaps some of us at this stage of the proceedings were beginning to tire—just a little—of each other's profile !

The young subaltern officers who, day by day, led the vans of the various columns through the forest, were subjected to great nerve-strain, and bore the part patiently and bravely.

We were thankful therefore to emerge again into the more open country and drink the cool and clear waters of the many streamlings bickering down the fertile valleys to swell the Sanaga, the river of many waterfalls that plunge into their roaring cauldrons and throw off clouds of silver spray—"pictures of beauty and power framed in luxuriant tropical vegetation"; feast our eyes upon fragrant flowering shrubs and plants exquisite in their varied tints, and, above all, to receive friendly greetings from the natives, who, no sooner had the Germans retired, crept from hiding-places to reoccupy their villages in which they hoped to dwell again in peace. Back to the land that supplied them bountifully with all that an

" PICTURES OF POWER "

African's heart and stomach could desire ; to a soil of surprising fertility, producing grain and vegetables a hundredfold, the tillage of which appeared to be done in an antiquated manner, chiefly by scantily clothed women wearing little false tails, who were not in the least abashed at the inquisitive gaze of the soldiers.

The French columns under Colonel Mayer which had advanced from Eseka on 23rd November, fought their way through the same old forest against the same determined opposition under practically the same conditions as we had experienced, losing many officers and men, their tenacity of purpose and fine spirit being, in the end, rewarded by the assault and capture of Mangeles, twenty-two miles south of Dschang-Mangas, on 21st December. Here they, too, halted to rest and refresh the troops and establish a new depot.

We must now for the present take leave of Dobell's columns at Dschang-Mangas and Mangeles and join up again with Cunliffe's northern force, which at the end of October was on the line Tibati–Banyo–Bamenda, but although the town of Banyo was in Cunliffe's hands, he discovered that a very strong position in the mountain

TILLING THE SOIL

near by was held by the enemy, and he realised that until this position was taken, it would be imprudent to continue his southern drive.

Banyo mountain, an isolated feature rising steeply above the surrounding rugged country, is covered with huge boulders, many of which had been connected by sangars, and every salient had been fortified. In short, this mountain had been selected by the Germans as a rallying-point for their garrisons of the central plateau and equipped and provisioned to withstand a prolonged siege.

By 2nd November, Cunliffe had assembled his infantry (four and a half companies and ten machine-guns) along the under features of the mountain and disposed his mounted infantry widely around the base to give him timely warning of any attempt on the part of the enemy to break through.

The attack was delivered early on the morning of 4th November. " The positions on the mountain looked grim and stupendous," wrote an officer who was present. The infantry, covered by the fire of three of our mountain guns, worked their way upwards over rocks and boulders and through the high grass and thorny scrub ; exposed to severe rifle and machine-gun fire, unflinchingly they went until checked at a line of sangars half-way up the mountain side, and though officers and men were exhausted and drenched by the rain, like good and seasoned soldiers they hung on to the ground they had won.

Captain C. G. Bowyer-Smijth, the Gloucester Regiment, hidden by the morning mist, had actually led his company right up to the crest, where it came suddenly under a severe cross fire, and Captain Bowyer-Smijth, an able and fearless officer, having been killed, his company was forced back for some distance. At dawn on the 5th, the attack was renewed, and the companies having reached the outer works of the main position, were subjected not only to heavy firing, but the rolling down of loose rocks and some bomb-throwing. All through that day, however, they continued the upward fight, capturing sangar after sangar, until at dusk they had all but completed their arduous job. The task of bringing up food and water to the firing line was most creditably performed by the transport carriers.

Darkness set in early that evening, and during the night a terrific thunderstorm burst over the mountain, but by the early morning of 6th December the fight was won— white flags were seen on the mountain-top, and our men silhouetted against the skyline. The enemy, completely demoralised, had broken up into small parties, and aided by darkness and the din of the tempest, had wormed their way down the mountain only to be taken by our mounted infantry patrols on the plain below. It appears that the German commander on the evening of the 5th, seeing that the game was over, issued orders to his troops to try and get through the attackers and rendezvous at Ngambe. " This action," wrote General Cunliffe, " may, I think, be justly described as one of the most arduous ever fought by African troops."

In the meantime Lieut. Col. Cotton's Column, known as the Bare Column, from General Dobell's Command, consisting of 3 companies 5th Indian Light Infantry, 2

BANYO MOUNTAIN CAPTURED BY GENERAL CUNLIFFE'S TROOPS,
6.12.1915

companies West African Regiment, and 2 mountain guns, in all about 500 rifles, had moved up from Bare, and after stubborn fighting in the mountains between Mbo and Dschang occupied the latter place on 6th November.

With regard to the further movements of this column I quote from the diary of Colonel C. S. Stooks, D.S.O., who took part in the operation :

" On 24th November a portion of this column—roughly half, the rest having been left to garrison Dschang—and a column of Waffs (Nigerians of the West African Frontier Force under Major Crookenden), with which it had joined hands a few days before at Bagam, found themselves held

up at the Nun river on the road to Fumban by a German
column. This column was the late garrison of Bagam,
which, having left that place before our troops arrived,
had succeeded in getting its main portion across the river
in comfort. Its rearguard had, however, given us a good
deal of scrapping.

" The river, running north and south, was deep, broad,
and of a strong current, and the Germans had removed
and burnt all boats : no ford or other means of crossing
existed.

" In order, therefore, to solve the conundrum of getting

ARRIVAL OF GERMAN GOVERNOR AT BANYO (PRE-WAR)

to Fumban, the two column commanders had agreed on
the following plan :

" Crookenden and his Waffs were to return on their tracks
and make a wide turning movement to the north, cross
the river near its head waters, and then turn south and
come in at the rear of the enemy opposing us. This
turning movement would take the best part of six days,
good marchers though the Waffs are, as the distance was
anything up to 120 miles.

" Meanwhile we—the Bare Column—were to keep the
enemy amused, replenish our scanty supplies, and get some
rafts or boats made locally with a view to an eventual
crossing.

Q

" The Waffs moved off on this long trek on the 25th, and we settled down to our part of the show.

" Our hopes of a few days' ' make and mend ' were, however, soon dispelled. The disturber of our peace was not the German commander from across the river, who contented himself with an occasional ' hate ' when stirred up by our picquets, but was a deputation from the king of Fumban. The envoy arrived under a flag of truce and brought greetings from his master and a request that we would advance on Fumban as quickly as possible. The message continued that the Germans were leaving Fum-

BANYO STATION DURING GERMAN OCCUPATION

ban ; that they had already hanged some of his chief men, and he (the king) feared the worst for himself ; that the envoy knew of a place up stream which was not watched by the Germans, and where our force could cross ; that any food we wanted should be forthcoming once we were over his border (the Nun), and please would we come quickly.

" The fact of the proposed crossing-place being up stream enabled the column commander to fall in with the king's views, as such a move would only mean that we should meet the Waff column one or two days earlier than ex- pected, and on the left or German bank of the river.

Moreover, the Germans had not shown any signs of an offensive spirit, so there seemed little danger in leaving the crossing lightly guarded.

" The O.C. Wars was therefore ordered to leave an officer and twenty-five men at the crossing to keep the enemy amused and to receive and cherish our expected convoy, while the remainder of the column, i.e. the Indian regiment and the rest of the Wars, with the gun, would trust itself to the guidance of the envoy and hope for the best.

" The Wars therefore started off that night—the 26th

THE BANYO BAND

—guided by the envoy in person, while we followed early the next morning, led by one of his assistants.

" Never shall I forget that march !

" The road led over some high ground near the crossing, and as this was the only spot where our movements would be visible to the enemy, it had to be negotiated before daylight. Consequently, 4 a.m. was fixed on for the start, and an hour later we were safely past the danger spot and swallowed up in the swamp fringing the river. In this swamp we continued for the next seven hours.

" The bright spots on that day are marked in my memory by the rare occasions on which we touched dry land. For the most part, when we were not tripping over creepers in the darkness, we were falling into mud-holes ; when we were not up to our waists in mud-holes we were knocking our heads against overhanging branches. How the gun-carriers managed to get their loads along passes the imagination ; but they are truly marvellous fellows, these Sierra Leone carriers, and can do most things which require strength and endurance.

" At last we emerged from our marshy jungle on to a nice open bit of swamp with a small hill growing out of it. This hill our guide indicated as marking the crossing-place.

" The Wars had arrived an hour or so before, and had already sent an officer and a few men across the river in the only two available boats. The envoy had gone with them to procure more boats from the Fumban side.

" The hill proved to be the only dry place for miles—a veritable oasis in a waste of swamp, and boasted a narrow beach at its base on which we could settle the men down. The next thing was to see about getting the army over, and fortunately the envoy soon arrived at the head of a fleet of a dozen more boats.

" These boats we were destined to know well in the next few days. The word boat is an entire misnomer—raft would be better—but semi-buoyant faggot describes them best. The motive power is provided by a native with a long pole.

" We found that not more than three men with their rifles and kit could safely be put on the best of these con-traptions, and as we had some 250 fighting men and a large army of carriers, besides kit, ammunition, a gun and Maxims, and a certain amount of supplies, the crossing took some time. Moreover, the opposite landing-place was a mile and a half up stream, and our archaic craft took the best part of three hours to do the return journey ; so it was not till the evening of the 29th that the last of the troops and stores were over.

" The nature of the river was such that work could only

be done by daylight : as soon as the sun set an impenetrable mist closed down, and one unfortunate European sergeant of the Wars (Sergeant Elvey), who crossed late, spent the night on his half-submerged raft surrounded by bellowing

TWO VIEWS OF MBO FORT (CAPTURED BY OUR TROOPS, 31.12.1914, AND AGAIN IN OCTOBER 1915)

hippos, owing to the failure of his boatman to find the landing-place.

" We were now on the German side of the river, twelve miles or so above the main crossing where the enemy was patiently waiting for us, and it only remained to get into touch with Crookenden and his Waffs and arrange a new plan of operations. The envoy, who was now on his own

ground, had not been idle, and had sent out various myr-
midons to look for Crookenden ; in due course they found
him, and the following plan was agreed upon by the two
column commanders :

" The Waffs were to continue their march to the main
crossing, and were then to fall on the enemy from behind,
release our detachment and eke our convoy. Their further
movements would be governed by circumstances. As a
matter of fact, after a good
deal of scrapping, they released   our   convoy   and
finally occupied Kuti, ten
miles south of Fumban, on
5th December.

" We, the Bare Column,
were to make the best of
our way to Fumban by a
side road and relieve the
king from his anxieties.

" We therefore proceeded
to carry out our part of the
programme, and, after burning a German military post
—the greater part of the
garrison of which was hunt-
ing for the Waff Column in
quite the wrong direction—
found ourselves, early on 2nd December, approaching the
walled city of Fumban, the capital of the native state of
Bamun.

A CHIEF OF THE HINTERLAND

" The town is protected by two systems of defences with
certain roughly-defined entrances.   The outer line consists of a very high mound and deep ditch enclosing a
huge tract of country as well as the town proper.   This
mound could be seen away in the distance taking the hills
and valleys as they came, and its total length must be
anything up to thirty-five miles. The king told me that

it was made by his grandfather ninety years ago, before a white man had ever been heard of in the country. The inner line of defence surrounds the town proper and, like the outer one, consists of a formidable mound and ditch. The main road from the Nun, on which we now were, enters it by a solidly built gateway with guard-houses and loop-holed towers.

" As the column was nearing the inner wall a messenger was seen to be approaching : he proved to be an emissary from the king to say that his sable majesty was on the point of arriving, and at the next turn in the road we came face to face with the cavalcade.

REED RAFTS ON THE NUN RIVER

" The king himself and one or two of his courtiers were mounted on ponies—the rest of the suite was on foot.

" The column halted, and the column commander awaited the arrival of the king, who hurriedly threw himself off his pony and advanced on foot—a fine upstanding man, not very negro in type, dressed in blue robes and wearing a turban with the end tied under his chin and over his mouth.

" He was a trifle nervous, as he did not know what to expect, but on being told that no harm would come to him he brightened up and told us that the German troops had left the town the day before.

" As to supplies, the recital made our mouths water—

beef, goats, fowls, ' duck-fowls,' ' hen-fruit ' (the words are the king's), bananas and pineapples brought visions of better times to men who for the last ten days had been existing and marching eight to ten hours daily on a scanty diet.

" At last we arrived at the king's village, which was approached by a large and sombre-looking gateway guarded by a selection of burly ruffians armed with bows and arrows and broad-bladed spears.

" At some little distance from the gatehouse was a gigantic flagstaff near which the king and his court had taken up their position surrounded by his subjects.

A HEFTY PUNTER, NUN RIVER

" Our travel-stained and ragged army then marched in and took up its position facing the flagstaff. A small Union Jack was bent on to the halyards, run up, and broken out. The troops presented arms, and the only two buglers with the force sounded the General Salute. As the flag rose the assembled natives, at a sign from the king, clapped their hands, making a great volume of sound. The army then sloped arms and, the column commander having called· for three cheers for His Majesty King George V, Fumban became, temporarily at any rate, a portion of the British Empire.

The king now hurried off with the Staff to arrange for our accommodation in the late German barracks on the northern spur of the ridge, while the troops fell out and I doubt not allowed their thoughts to wander to the flesh-pots of Fumban. But it was not to be—in this case there was a very big slip—for a letter was brought to the king addressed to the late German commandant. It was from one Losch—a German column commander—and stated that he proposed to enter the town in the course of the next hour or so. He evidently knew nothing of our arrival. Hard on the heels of this messenger came another from Major Uniacke commanding a Nigerian column from Banyo, saying that he also was about to arrive and bidding the king prepare for him. This made matters simple, as Uniacke could look after the town while we went out to strafe Losch.

" Arrangements were soon completed, but the Germans

THE FUMBAN LADIES' ORCHESTRA

had too good a start, and all we got were a few wounded prisoners, four or five ponies, some rifles and several boxes of ammunition.

" The chase was continued for a mile or so with no further result than the probable one of having given Losch's column the surprise of its life and scattering it to the four winds.

" That night I had a bath and dined off a ' duck-fowl ' in the German barracks.

" The next week was occupied in clearing up the country and making ourselves comfortable and safe for a possibly protracted stay.

" The king, Njoya, appears to be quite an enlightened man except in the matter of his matrimonial affairs. Here he has slipped up badly, as he has six hundred wives and one hundred and forty-nine children—and owns to thirty-six years of age !

" He holds a daily durbar outside the gatehouse for the dispensing of justice and receipt of tribute, and all and sundry seem to have access to him. But there is a very well-defined code of court etiquette observed. Any courtier wishing to speak to him assumes a cringing attitude, removes his skull-cap, clasps his hands and, taking a chukker round behind the presence, finally arrives at the royal elbow. Here he averts his head and makes his request in a hoarse whisper. When the king coughs or clears his throat everyone present softly claps his hands.

" One day the column commander and I visited Njoya in his house. This is built on the European pattern and was garnished with cheap German furniture. A large photograph of Njoya in a special German uniform, including a pickelhaube, adorns one wall of his room ; an equal-sized portrait of his chief wife graces the other. An empty photograph frame stood on the table, and Njoya naïvely explained that it had contained a portrait of the Kaiser but that now he proposed to substitute one of King George.

" Soon after these events the Bare Column left Fumban on its return journey to Dschang, where it split up into its component parts, the Indian regiment shortly after leaving the country to take part in another side-show elswhere."

Captain C. S. Burt, D.S.O., South Staffordshire Regiment, who was Supply and Transport Officer with Colonel Cotton's column, told me that after Mbo fort had been retaken by our troops, it became necessary to recruit natives from the local tribes as carriers for the further advance northwards, and that on the first day's march, in order to get the carriers gradually into good condition, he gave them light loads consisting of cases of "bully beef," which was used to supplement the troops' rice ration when no fresh meat was procurable. At the end of the first day's march, when checking the loads, he discovered that several cases of the beef were missing, and as the headman of the carrier corps could give no satisfactory explanation and denied all knowledge of the loss, it was decreed that as the amount of beef which had undoubtedly been stolen equalled two days' supply, the carriers concerned would receive no issue for that of the following day. Being well fortified, however, with the missing beef, which was voted a rare delicacy by the natives, they accepted the Transport Officer's judgment as fair and just in the circumstances. The following morning, as was his daily practice, Captain Burt mounted his pony and rode along the transport column, where all appeared to be going well, the carriers plodding steadily forward under their loads.

KING OF FUMBAN WITH ONE OF THE SIX HUNDRED

Knowing that the Transport Officer was a very generous and cheery soul, and hoping his heart might have been softened since the perpetration of the crime, at the end of that day's march they paraded at the ration dump, hoping to receive their rations as usual, but the "try on" failed. The next day all were present and cheerful, but as Captain Burt rode along the column, there seemed to be something missing which for a time he could not call to mind. Then it suddenly dawned upon him that the pack of pariah dogs which had followed the troops from the villages on the line of march

1. TRANSPORT CARRIERS ON MARCH
2. THE LONG BAGGAGE COLUMN
3. DUMPING THE LOADS

had disappeared. The carriers carried the day ! They had their meat ration after all—but it was not tinned !

After the capture of Banyo, Fumban and Tibati, General Cunliffe continued the southward drive against steady resistance, and by 18th December his columns had occupied the line Yoko–Linte–Ditam.

CHAPTER XII

REVERTING to the operation of the main (Duala) force, on hearing that the British contingent had gained its first objective, Dschang-Mangas, on 17th December, 1915, General Dobell, appreciating the importance of an early occupation of Yaunde, decided to move it forthwith on that place rather than wait until the French were ready to continue their advance from Mangeles. Consequently, on 23rd December, having replenished supplies and completed a good temporary hospital within a strong post, my columns were again set in motion eastwards. Stubbornly opposed, we made little headway at first. On Christmas Eve we found, on the main road, a message from the enemy Commander conveying "greetings to our gallantly fighting enemies," suggesting a cessation of hostilities for the festive season and concluding : "We *will* have our *Christmas*, and don't you forget it!" But these overtures were not favourably entertained and we pressed forward with unabated vigour, gaining on Christmas Day a line astride the main road about twenty miles from our goal. Continuing the pressure on the 26th against a resistance now perceptibly weakening, a succession of strongly entrenched positions were hastily abandoned by the retreating enemy. On 31st December, 1915, our main body and British Headquarters were at Fimba, three and a half miles west of Yaunde fort, the left detachment under Major F. Anderson at Makenge and the right flank column under Lieut. Col.

H. de B. Rose at Mendong astride the Yaunde–Kribi
road. We held a frontage of about six miles, and favourable positions from which to reconnoitre and issue orders
for an assault. But there were no signs of enemy activity ;
the natives were beginning to creep cautiously from hiding-
places and peep through the bushes, and enemy soldiers
were surrendering to our patrols ; all evidence that
they were at last on the run and the fighting finished.
Our Sedan in miniature was not to be and the
appetites of the field-force fire-eaters were, after all, to go

DISTANT VIEW OF YAUNDE FORT, CAPTURED BY BRITISH TROOPS,
1.1.1916

unsated ! And so, on New Year's Day, 1916, on the heels
of the German rear-guard, my columns entered Yaunde,
and by sunset on that day the fort and all the surrounding
hills were ours. Yaunde, the promised land of which we
had heard so much, was in reality a disappointing, dismal
spot, made up of isolated settlements including mission
stations, hospitals, official residences, barracks, fort, etc.,
perched on hills and ridges covered with high grass and
bush with wide clearings for gardens and cultivation, the
hill-sides dotted with an old African friend, the lonely
elephantine Baobab. We found nothing in this deserted
place either to eat, to drink, or to play with, and by way

of adding insult to injury they left it in a most insanitary condition, dangerous to the health of our troops. However, under the guidance of Major Booth, our Assistant Director of Medical Services, it was soon transformed into a pleasant garden city in which could be heard the cheerful voices of the African soldiers and carriers echoing across the hills.

The day we entered Yaunde (1st January, 1916) General Cunliffe's troops were hastening southwards from the line Ngila–Ndenge, and by 8th January had not only joined hands with General Aymerich's French and

ELEPHANTINE BAOBABS

Belgian columns now pouring in from the east, but had arrived on the Sanaga river and secured its main crossing at the Nachtigal falls, forty miles north of Yaunde. Here Cunliffe learned that the place was in our hands. His task was therefore practically ended ; his troops had covered great distances, having marched continuously for over 600 miles through mountainous country intersected by deep ravines and tropical rivers, and some of the positions they had won were of almost impregnable natural strength, reinforced by German military science. Colonel Brisset's French column, which had joined Cunliffe's command early in the campaign, and which arrived in

Yaunde on 9th January, had actually marched and fought for over 1000 miles, a fine feat of arms.

Colonel Brisset's letter announcing his arrival is here reproduced.

General Aymerich with the troops from French Equatorial Africa arrived in Yaunde on 8th January after many months of strenuous campaigning by river, swamp, jungle and forest during which they received and gave many hard knocks. They all looked wonderfully well and as hard as nails after their great effort. It was a pleasure to meet General Aymerich, his distinguished officers and

"KIDDIES" OF THE MISSION   THE MISSION STATION, YAUNDE

brave troops, and to offer him on behalf of the British contingent very sincere congratulations.

And there is a little bit of jam in the form of a telegram from Colonel Mayer, Commandant of the French contingent based on Eseka, much appreciated by one and all.

Colonel Gorges   Jaunde

Je vous adresse à vous et aux officiers de la colonne anglaise toute nos felicitations au sujet de la prise de Jaunde

Signe Mayer Eseka

Le 3 janvier 1916

The Germans who had evacuated Yaunde under pressure from all sides, headed south-west for Spanish Guinea, about 130 miles distant, and Allied columns sent in pursuit failed to bring them to action. On 8th January,

R

1916, there was a rear-guard affair near Kolmaka on the Nyong river, when Lieut. Col. Haywood, whom I had

COLONEL BRISSET'S LETTER

despatched from Yaunde on the 5th with a light column, obtained the release of all our prisoners of war, amongst them being some British and French officers and civilians, native soldiers and a few non-combatants who had been taken by the Germans at various stages of the campaign. All had received fair and humane treatment during their captivity.

By 18th January the remnants of the enemy forces were in full retreat and, in spite of all the elaborate and carefully laid plans made to intercept them, they managed to slip through the meshes of the Allied net into neutral territory where, early in February 1916, Herr Ebermaier the Governor, Colonel Zimmermann, the Commander of the troops, and a large number of Germans and natives surrendered to the Spanish authorities. A little later on the Germans were transported to Spain and interned. A good many of their native troops had melted away before the neutral territory was reached.

As the fortress of Mora, in the extreme north of the colony, still held out, an ultimatum was despatched by General Cunliffe to its Commander, Hauptmann von Raben, offering the following liberal terms in case of surrender : Officers to be permitted to retain their swords, all Europeans to be sent to England as prisoners of war, and the native soldiers of the garrison to be given safe passages to their homes. These terms were at once accepted, and with the capitulation of Mora on 18th February, 1916, the conquest of the Cameroons was completed and Germany dispossessed of all her West African colonies.

The health of the troops, especially of those engaged in the coastal regions, was a constant cause of anxiety, not only to the General commanding, but to the Director of Medical Services, Colonel J. C. B. Statham, C.M.G., C.B.E., and his medical staff, to whom one and all were deeply grateful for the manful way in which they faced and handled and triumphed over enormous difficulties, and, above all, for the great care and kindness with which they tended the sick and wounded, Europeans and natives alike, throughout the campaign. The medical services were organised under unusual conditions, as the medical units were hurriedly created at sea from the personnel picked up at the various West African ports. They were composed mainly of medical officers of the West African Medical Staff, with a varied assortment of equipment. It was manifestly impossible to collect reliable medical statistics from the numerous moving columns widely separated over so vast an area, but actual figures of the forces based on Duala are available and were obtained

GERMANS IN YAUNDE FORT (PRE-WAR DAYS)

from an analysis of 24,000 in-patients and 25,000 out-patients treated at the base hospital. The most remarkable fact shown by these figures is the number of cases of tropical ulcers, which formed 25 per cent or 6000 of the in-patients, and 50 per cent or 12,500 of the out-patients. This baneful malady spread so rapidly that it became almost epidemic in the nature of its increase and proved so difficult to cure as to render those affected unfit for service for several weeks, and unless the ulcers received early treatment, invaliding was found to be the soundest policy to adopt. Of specific diseases, malaria came first, and the

Map to illustrate
THE CAMPAIGN IN THE
CAMEROONS 1914-1916
Scale of Miles
50 40 30 20 10 0   50   100

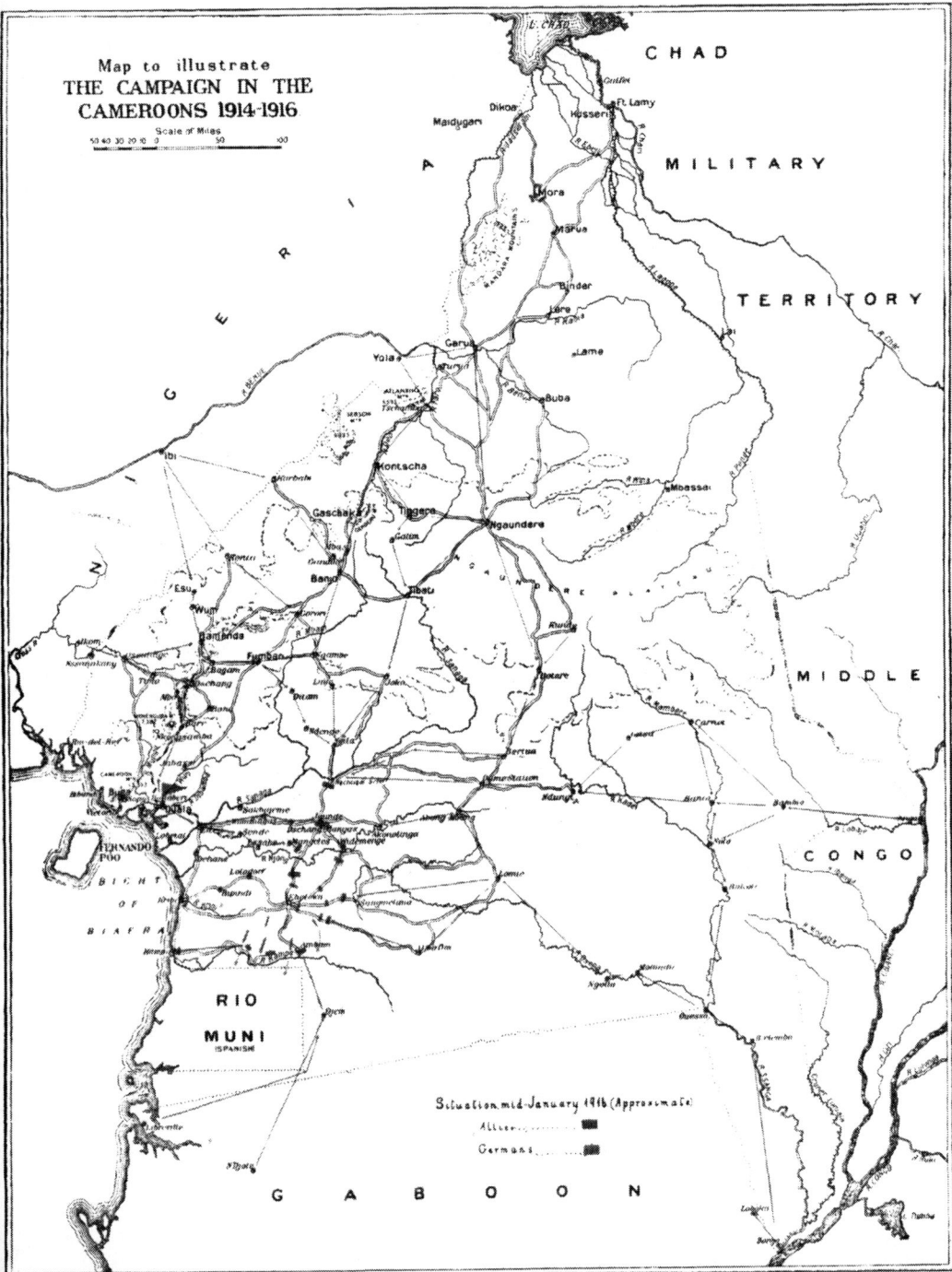

L. CHAD
CHAD
Guifei
Ft. Lamy
Maidugari
Dikoa
Kasseri
MILITARY
Mora
TERRITORY
Marua
Binder
Lere
Garua
Lama
Yola
Buba
Ibi
Kontscha
Mbassai
Gaschaka
Tingere
Gatan
Ngaundere
MIDDLE
Esu
Banjo
Tibati
Wum
Bamenda
Rundu
Foumban
Batare
CONGO
Kusseri
CAMEROON
Duala
FERNANDO
POO
BIGHT
OF
BIAFRA
RIO
MUNI
(SPANISH)
GABOON

Situation mid-January 1916 (Approximate)
Allies
Germans

Duala hospital admissions give no idea of its prevalence amongst Europeans as the greatest number were attacked whilst in the field, where they were treated in temporary bush huts or in the field ambulance shelters. Of some 3000 Europeans serving with the force, many had over a dozen malarial attacks during the eighteen months of the campaign, while scarcely any escaped altogether. From General Dobell's force alone 150 Europeans were invalided for this disease.

Dysentery caused 2000 admissions to the base hospital,

TYPICAL COUNTRY THROUGH WHICH GENERAL CUNLIFFE'S COLUMNS
FOUGHT

of whom 176 died and 1000 natives and 50 Europeans were invalided. During the rainy season pneumonia was rife, there being 800 cases of whom 500 were invalided and 150 died. Rheumatism also caused great wastage, nearly 4000 cases, of whom some 400 were invalided, and then there was beri-beri, chiefly among the French troops, which was attributed to the use of rice imported from Cochin China. And so the story of disease and suffering could be continued, but enough has perhaps been said to show what officers and men endured in addition to the battle casualties, which, all things considered, were comparatively slight. The total admissions to hospitals inclusive of transport carriers from all the various columns must have exceeded 35,000, the figures for the Duala hospital alone being, as stated, over 24,000. The approximate battle casualties, including killed, wounded, and died of disease, were 4600. According to the reports of the X-ray laboratory at the Duala hospital, bullets of various calibre and structure had been used by the enemy, from the military nickel to the soft-nosed and large lead bullets of old pattern police and sporting rifles, and the serious and terrible nature of some of the wounds inflicted

EUROPEAN HOSPITAL, DUALA

by the soft-nosed and lead, usually at very close ranges, caused a good deal of unnecessary suffering to our troops.

So we see that even in an African side-show, *Es ist der krieg ein roh gewaltsam handwerk.*[1] But with all its violence and destructiveness it was voted by many to be a glorious and strenuous life and an excellent schooling of the heart.

Cameroons under the mandate was apportioned to France and Great Britain, the former claiming and receiving the lion's share, including Duala, the capital and chief port, whilst to the latter was handed over the coast settlement of Victoria together with a narrow strip of territory adjoining Nigeria and containing most of the

[1] *Schiller.*

great mountain chain, including Cameroon mountain, one of the great landmarks of Africa.

Apart from the invaluable services rendered by sea, creek, river, and land by the British and French naval forces under their respective commanders, Captain Cyril Fuller and Capitaine de Vaisseau Carré and the officers and men of the Nigerian Marine, some 8000 British, 10,000 French and 600 Belgian troops with at least 40,000 transport carriers, had been employed. The rank and file, save for the Indian Regiment (5th Light Infantry) and a detachment of the West India Regiment, being all

YAUNDE CLUB, USED BY GERMANS AS AN AMMUNITION FACTORY

natives of West or Central Africa. Concerning the bearing of these troops, much has already been said, but before closing the book and in fairness to all, these few words must be added : That in spite of a bad start, some early reverses and a few " incidents," both officers and men greatly distinguished themselves, the former by their leading and example, the latter by their attachment to and trust in their officers. One of the brightest memories of the campaign will ever be their wondrous patience and cheerfulness under all circumstances. We must remember, too, that they never quite understood what all the trouble was about. They neither grasped the true significance of the stupendous feud that was waging, nor the consequences of victory or defeat to the future of their country. Yet they endured great privations, and did their utmost to help to put the King's enemies under subjection. Looting and ill-treatment of the inhabitants of the colony were practically unknown throughout the conflict, which speaks volumes for the discipline of the force.

With regard to the Commands and Staffs, mistakes there were and " set-backs," as indeed there were bound to be in such a country and climate and against an enemy well led, trained and hardened to bush and forest fighting. There was perhaps, at times, a tendency to set too high a value on his fighting qualities and to overestimate his strength—in fact, too much playing for safety—but all things considered, the operations were well conceived and skilfully executed, the commanding Generals, Dobell (in chief command), Aymerich, and Cunliffe, working in harmony, brought a long-drawn-out campaign, beset with great difficulties, to a successful issue, thereby regaining in some measure our prestige in Africa, which, following reverses in nearly every theatre, had been perceptibly waning. So bouquets were handed up, and no bricks thrown !

And what of the enemy ? To be silent would be un-generous. Against overwhelming odds, hemmed in on all sides by land and sea forces, with little hope of succour from the Fatherland, they fought a valiant fight. Their pluck, their endurance, their ingenuity, never wavered. With little artillery, with failing supplies of food and munitions, the inhabitants of the colony often up against them, they dealt us some punishing blows, and the manner in which the native soldiers stuck to their German officers until the hopelessness of the position became apparent, was one of the surprises of the campaign. All honour, then, to the German commander, his officers and men.

That is the end of the Tropical Tale, with its attendant pleasures and pains, and after nearly three years' continuous service on the " Coast," I, for one, was glad to walk down the sloping Duala road to the harbour landing-stage and board the homeward-bound mail steamer, followed by my orderly and soldier-servant, Momo, who thought nothing of waking me up in the middle of the night merely to ask the time or to plead for six months' advance of pay for " *Chop sah, for me famboly na Sally Own !* "[1] Dropping down the estuary to the open sea, one's thoughts turned intuitively towards the splendid fellows left behind—the

GERMAN GOVERNOR, HERR EBERMAIER, AND STAFF IN FULL WAR PAINT (PRE-WAR DAYS)

officers and non-commissioned officers resting in ever-lasting peace on mountain-sides and in secluded vales of Africa, those in whom love of country burned like a flame even amid conditions and surroundings at times difficult and hard to bear, those who lit the beacons on our way that we might see.

> " So, when our eventide fades into night,
>   Along the broken track of hopes and fears,
>   God grant that we may keep throughout the years
>   Their lamp alight."
>   *Hamish Hemington Mathams.*

And as our good ship, after rounding Cape Cameroon,

[1] For food for my family in Sierra Leone.

sped westwards on even keel, through the unruffled waters of the Bight, and the great Cameroon mountain slowly dropped behind the horizon, I heard the Coast calling me back again. My answer was, " No, not this journey. I'm homeward-bound to a l'il ole Island set in the silver sea I like better than any old coast ! "

COAST CALLING

APPENDIX I

NAVAL FORCES

(British and French)

CAMEROONS, 1914–1916

SHIP	DESCRIP-TION	COMMANDING OFFICER	TONS	I.H.P.	GUNS
H.M.S. *Cumberland*	Cruiser	Captain C. T. M. Fuller, Senior Naval Officer, Duala	9,800	22,000	14 6-inch 8 12-pdr. 3 3-pdr.
H.M.S. *Challenger*	Cruiser	Captain C. P. Beaty-Pownall	5,880	12,500	11 6-inch 8 12-pdr. 1 3-pdr.
H.M.S. *Astræa*	Cruiser	Captain A. C. Sykes	4,360	7,000	2 6-inch 8 4·7-inch 8 12-pdr. 1 3-pdr.
H.M.S. *Sirius*	Cruiser	Commander (Rtd.) W. H. Boys	3,600	7,000	4 6-inch 4 12-pdr. 1 3-pdr.
H.M.S. *Rinaldo*	Gunboat	Lieut. Commander H. M. Garrett	980	1,400	4 4-inch 4 3-pdr.
H.M.S. *Dwarf*	Gunboat	Commander F. E. K. Strong	710	900	2 4-inch 4 12-pdr.
Ivy	Nigerian Government Yacht	Commander (R.N.R.) R. H. W. Hughes			1 12-pdr. 2 6-pdr.
Pothuau	Croiseur Cuirassé	Capt. de Vaisseau J. A. Chéron	5,374	10,000	2 7·6-inch 10 5·5-inch 10 3-pdr.
Bruix	Croiseur Cuirassé	Comdt. de Vaisseau M. E. Tirard	4,735	8,700	2 7·6-inch 6 5·5-inch 4 9-pdr. 2 3-pdr. 6 1-pdr.
Friant	Croiseur	Capt. de Vaisseau E. F. Carré	3,882	9,500	6 6·5-inch 4 3·9-inch 8 3-pdr.

SHIP	DESCRIP-TION	COMMANDING OFFICER	TONS	I.H.P.	GUNS
Surprise	Canon-nière	Lieut. de Vaisseau Mégissier	617	900	2 4-inch 4 9-pdr. 4 1-pdr.
Amerique	Canon-nière	Enseigne de Vaisseau R. L. S. Joneaux	700	740	1 ·65 3 ·47
Vauban	Canon-nière	Lieut. de Vaisseau J. B. Boissarie	600	500	2 3-pdr.
Loiret	Transport	Lieut. de Vaisseau R. Chastang	—	1,050	2 ·47

AUXILIARY CRAFT
Manned from British Ships and Nigerian Marine

VESSEL	COMMANDING OFFICER	GUNS	REMARKS
Margaret Elizabeth	Commander R. S. Sneyd, R.N.	2 12-pdr.	Govt. Yacht, captured from enemy.
Fullah	Lieut. F. J. Lambert, R.N.	4 12-pdr.	Small transport, Nigerian Marine.
Sokoto	Chief Boatswain T. R. Clynick	1 3-pdr.	Stern-wheel gun-boat, captured from enemy.
Remus	Lieut. P. D. Henderson, R.N.R.	3 12-pdr.	Steam tug, Nigerian Marine.
Porpoise	Lieut. A. R. P. Martin, R.N.R.	2 12-pdr.	do.
Lagos	Lieut. J. A. Jones, R.N.R.	2 3-pdr.	Small transports, Nigerian Marine.
Uromi	Lieut. W. Maddison, R.N.R.	2 3-pdr.	do.
Sir Hugh	Lieut. J. S. Cave, R.N.R.	2 3-pdr.	do.
Sir Frederick	Lieut. F. J. Lambert, R.N.	2 3-pdr.	do.
Lala	Lieut. H. W. T. Pausey, R.N.	1 Maxim	do.
Anna Woër-mann	Lieut. D. R. Mason, R.N.R.	—	Transport, captured from enemy.

In addition to the above there were two steam-tugs, *Balbus* and *Walrus*, two 100-ft. motor-launches, *Alligator* and *Crocodile*, two 80-ft. steam-launches, *Vampire* and *Vigilant*, all armed with light guns and Maxims from the ships-of-war and manned by the Nigerian Marine.

There were also the dredger *Mole*, and a steel lighter, *Dreadnought*, on each of which was mounted a 6-inch gun from H.M.S. *Challenger*, and manned by gun-crews from that ship.

APPENDIX II

OFFICERS, WEST AFRICAN REGIMENT, JULY, 1914

Commandant.

Bt. Col. E. H. Gorges, D.S.O.

Lieutenant Colonel.

Lieut. Col. A. G. W. Grant.

Majors.

Major E. Vaughan, Manchester Regiment.
Major F. S. de M. Maude.
Major E. L. Cowie, West India Regiment.
Major J. P. Law, Devonshire Regiment.
Major L. G. W. Dobbin, Northamptonshire Regiment.

Captains.

Capt. M. C. L. Caulfeild-Stoker, Scottish Rifles.
Capt. E. S. Brand, Royal Fusiliers.
Capt. F. T. Williams, Northamptonshire Regiment.
Capt. R. D. Keyworth, Oxford and Bucks Light Infantry.
Capt. W. S. Rich, Cheshire Regiment.
Capt. H. M. Powell, South Staffordshire Regiment.
Capt. C. H. Dinnen, Liverpool Regiment.
Capt. A. C. Taylor, Scottish Rifles.
Capt. W. F. G. Willes, Dorest Regiment (Adjt.).
Capt. D. R. C. D. O'Flynn, Liverpool Regiment.
Capt. G. R. Fielding, Notts and Derbyshire Regiment.
Capt. J. R. Robertson, Bedfordshire Regiment.
Capt. J. S. M. Corrie, Scottish Rifles.

Subalterns.

Lieut. W. S. Browne, East Yorkshire Regiment.
Lieut. C. Pease, North Lancashire Regiment.
Lieut. C. H. B. Pridham, West India Regiment.
Lieut. W. M. Richardson, Duke of Cornwall's Light Infantry (*Asst. Adjt.*).
Lieut. J. H. S. Dimmer, King's Royal Rifle Corps.
Lieut. L. J. Jones, West India Regiment.
Lieut. E. G. Redway, Royal Irish Regiment.

Lieut. G. O. T. Bagley, Middlesex Regiment.
Lieut. H. J. Minniken, West India Regiment.
Lieut. H. W. Dakeyne, Royal Warwick Regiment.
Lieut. G. J. B. E. Massy, Connaught Rangers.
Lieut. A. J. Scully, Manchester Regiment.
Lieut. E. R. Macpherson, West India Regiment.
Lieut. V. W. H. Venour, Leinster Regiment.
Lieut. R. D. Bennett, Middlesex Regiment.
Lieut. J. S. Porter, East Yorkshire Regiment.
Lieut. T. R. H. Criffiths, West India Regiment.
Lieut. A. W. G. Tomlins, West India Regiment.
Lieut. H. G. Garbett, West India Regiment.
Lieut. B. J. Thruston, Lincolnshire Regiment.
Lieut. R. J. A. Betham, Royal Sussex Regiment.
Lieut. J. A. Thompson, Royal Sussex Regiment.
Lieut. R. P. Wood, York and Lancaster Regiment.
Lieut. H. C. Marten, South Staffordshire Regiment.
Lieut. W. E. Walker, West India Regiment.
Lieut. B. G. Atkin, Manchester Regiment.
Lieut. D. H. Nicholson, Royal Scots.
Lieut. R. M. L. Scott, Cheshire Regiment.
Lieut. W. F. Matthews, South Wales Borderers.
Lieut. H. B. Holt, Royal Munster Fusiliers.
Lieut. C. S. Burt, South Staffordshire Regiment.
Lieut. E. S. W. Leach, East Surrey Regiment.
Lieut. R. A. F. Montanaro, East Surrey Regiment.
2nd Lieut. S. G. McBride, Norfolk Regiment.

Quarter-Master.

Quarter-Master (*Hon. Lt.*) H. W. Stratton.

APPENDIX III

WEST AFRICAN FRONTIER FORCE 1915
(*Administered by the Colonial Office*)

Inspector-General of the West African Frontier Force : Col. (*temp. Brig. Gen.*) C. M. Dobell, C.M.G., D.S.O., *p.s.c.* [*l.*], A.D.C.

Staff Officers : Major F. Jenkins, Coldstream Guards ; Major J. Brough, M.V.O., Royal Marine Artillery, *p.s.c.* (*G.S.O.*, 2nd grade)

NIGERIA REGIMENT

STAFF

Commandant : Lieut. Col. F. H. G. Cunliffe.

Gen. Staff Officer, 2nd grade : Capt. W. D. Wright, V.C., Royal West Surrey Regiment, *p.s.c.*

Staff Captain : Capt. C. R. U. Savile, Royal Fusiliers.

Officer attd. to Gen. Staff : Major H. G. Howell, R.A.

Staff Quarter-Master : Hon. Capt. in Army J. M. Simpson.

ARTILLERY
(2 Batteries)

Captains

1 Major C. F. S. Maclaverty, Royal Artillery.
2 Capt. G. Heygate, Royal Artillery.

Lieutenants

1 Capt. R. J. R. Waller, Royal Artillery.
1 Capt. A. A. Cummins, Royal Artillery.
1 Lieut. O. T. Frith, Royal Artillery.
  Lieut. O. G. Body, Royal Artillery.
  2nd Lieut. T. A. Vise, Royal Artillery.

INFANTRY (4 Battalions) and MOUNTED INFANTRY
(1 Battalion)

Lieut. Colonels

1 Major J. B. Cockburn, Royal Welch Fusiliers.
3 Major G. T. Mair, D.S.O., Royal Artillery.

2 Major A. H. W. Haywood, Royal Artillery (L.).
4 Bt. Major W. I. Webb-Bowen, Middlesex Regiment.

Major Comdg. M.I. Bn.

5 Capt. J. T. Gibbs, 3 D.G.

Majors

4 Capt. J. R. Heard, Shropshire Light Infantry.
2 Capt. R. W. Fox, Royal Warwickshire Regiment.
1 Major R. G. Coles, Suffolk Regiment.
2 Major G. D. Mann, Royal Artillery.

Captains

4 Hon. Major G. N. Sheffield, 3 Bn. Essex Regiment.
  Capt. C. C. West, Royal Highlanders.
1 Capt. H. W. Green, East Kent Regiment.
3 Capt. G. S. C. Adams, Royal West Surrey Regiment.
4 Capt. C. Gibb, Royal Scots Fusiliers.
2 *Capt. J. G. Gordon, Royal Irish Fusiliers, Adjt.*
2 Capt. E. C. Feneran, Royal West Surrey Regiment.
3 Capt. J. Crookenden, East Kent Regiment.
5 Capt. J. F. Badham, Worcestershire Regiment.
1 Capt. J. W. Chamley, Border Regiment.
3 Capt. N. W. Lawder, Bedfordshire Regiment.
4 Capt. J. Sargent, Lancashire Fusiliers.
3 Capt. J. A. Stewart, Royal Scots Fusiliers.
3 Capt. C. E. Roberts, Northamptonshire Regiment.
2 Capt. W. T. McG. Bate, West Riding Regiment.
2 Capt. R. S. S. Paton, East Surrey Regiment.
4 Capt. J. P. D. Underwood, North Lancashire Regiment.
1 Capt. B. Edwards, Royal Artillery.
4 Capt. A. H. L. Marwood, York and Lancaster Regiment.
1 *Capt. M. H. S. Willis, Suffolk Regiment, Adjt.*
2 Capt. B. C. Parr, Oxford and Bucks Light Infantry.
  Capt. A. W. Balders, Norfolk Regiment.
  Capt. N. P. Shand, Norfolk Regiment.
1 Capt. A. H. Giles, Gloucestershire Regiment.
(1) Capt. T. W. P. Dyer, Reserve of Officers.
(1) Capt. G. Seccombe, Reserve of Officers.
4 Capt. D. E. Wilson, Royal Dublin Fusiliers.
4 Capt. S. N. C. Webb, South Wales Borderers.
1 Capt. C. L. Waters, Royal Berkshire Regiment.
5 Capt. A. F. P. Knapp, North Lancashire Regiment.
1 Capt. C. P. L. Marwood, Royal Warwickshire Regiment.
1 Capt. C. M. H. Venour, Hampshire Regiment.
2 Capt. J. F. Thomson, North Staffordshire Regiment.
1 Capt. H. H. Kennedy, Seaforth Highlanders.

Lieutenants

(2) Capt. W. E. Beamish, 5 Bn. Royal Munster Fusiliers.
4 *Capt. O. F. R. Lenke, East Lancashire Regiment, Paymr.* and *Qr.-Mr.*
5 Capt. J. G. J. Kilkelly, Royal Munster Fusiliers.
Capt. F. J. H. Pring, Cheshire Regiment.
4 Capt. A. L. de C. Stretton, South Lancashire Regiment.
3 Capt. C. W. Meissner, Suffolk Regiment.
3 Capt. D. G. Gunn, Cheshire Regiment.
Capt. (*Hon. Lt. in Army*) G. E. S. Woodyatt, 4 Bn. Lancashire
    Fusiliers.
3 Capt. A. C. Milne-Home, Northumberland Fusiliers.
3 Capt. W. G. Yates, Royal West Kent Regiment.
2 *Capt. A. L. Wrenford, Worcestershire Regiment.*
3 Capt. K. G. F. Collins, Dorset Regiment.
1 Capt. J. G. Bruxner-Randall, Royal Welch Fusiliers.
3 Capt. W. Weatherbe, Royal Artillery.
2 Capt. C. H. Fowle, Hampshire Regiment.
2 Capt. E. A. Sandilands, Royal Scots Fusiliers.
2 Capt. E. R. M. Kirkpatrick, Yorkshire Light Infantry.
3 Capt. C. G. Bowyer-Smijth, Gloucestershire Regiment.
1 Capt. H. C. Fausset, North Staffordshire Regiment.
1 Capt. L. B. Paget, Rifle Brigade.
Capt. G. C. Sambidge, 4 Bn. Royal Warwick Regiment.
Capt. W. Stanford-Samuel, 4 Bn. Liverpool Regiment.
1 Capt. G. T. Burney, Gordon Highlanders.
Capt. J. S. P. Evans, 3 Bn. Cameron Highlanders.
4 *Capt. A. E. Beattie, Royal West Surrey Regiment, Adjt.*
1 Capt. C. Luxford, East Surrey Regiment.
5 Capt. J. H. G. Smyth, 3 Bn. Royal Munster Fusiliers.
4 Capt. C. A. Bradford, Yorkshire Regiment.
1 Capt. H. D. S. O'Brien, Northamptonshire Regiment.
4 Capt. C. R. Hetley, West Riding Regiment.
2 Capt. M. E. Fell, Connaught Rangers.
1 Capt. E. R. L. Maunsell, Royal Dublin Fusiliers.
5 Capt. L. N. A. Mackinnon, Coldstream Guards.
1 Capt. H. H. A. Cooke, Connaught Rangers.
3 Lieut. C. D. Harris, Shropshire Light Infantry.
3 Lieut. T. R. Umbers, Royal Irish Rifles.
5 Lieut. C. W. T. Lane, 7 Dragoon Guards.
4 Lieut. J. F. Warren, Durham Light Infantry.
1 Lieut. H. C. V. Porter, West India Regiment.
4 Lieut. J. E. H. Maxwell, Notts and Derby Regiment.
4 Lieut. J. K. B. Campbell, King's Own Scottish Borderers.
3 Lieut. J. G. Collins, Worcestershire Regiment.
2 Lieut. J. F. W. Allen, East Kent Regiment.
2 Lieut. R. Scott-Moncrieff, Royal Scots.
1 Lieut. C. S. Field, Worcestershire Regiment.
2 Lieut. H. C. T. Stronge, East Kent Regiment.
1 Lieut. L. C. Bostock, Manchester Regiment.

S

4 Lieut. K. S. Grove, York and Lancaster Regiment.
2 Lieut. G. G. Murray, York and Lancaster Regiment.
3 Lieut. A. C. Robinson, South Lancashire Regiment.
2 Lieut. G. E. Barclay, Royal Lancashire Regiment.
1 Lieut. A. F. Hordern, South Staffordshire Regiment.
2 Lieut. P. C. Higgins, Shropshire Light Infantry.
2 Lieut. E. E. Loch, Highland Light Infantry.
4 Lieut. T. P. Brawn, North Staffordshire Regiment.
1 Lieut. B. J. C. Dudley, Dorset Regiment.
2 Lieut. A. C. L. D. Lees, Shropshire Light Infantry.
4 Lieut. R. V. Burke, Connaught Rangers.
3 Lieut. R. R. Taylor, King's Own Scottish Borderers.
3 Lieut. R. M. Rodwell, Royal Irish Rifles.
　Temp. Lieut. W. G. E. Longworth, 7 (Serv.) Bn. Royal Irish
　　Fusiliers.
　Temp. Lieut. B. Roberts, 11 (Serv.) Bn. Gloucestershire Regiment.
　Lieut. A. W. Battersby, 4 Bn. Connaught Rangers.
　Temp. Lieut. J. P. W. Davies, 11 (Serv.) Bn. Gloucestershire Regi-
　　ment.
(1) Temp. Lieut. M. Whitworth.
(2) Temp. Lieut. E. L. Mort.
　2nd Lieut. (on prob.) H. E. Wightwick, 4 Bn. Scottish Rifles.
　2nd Lieut. R. J. Ramsey, 3 Bn. Royal Irish Rifles.
　2nd Lieut. J. T. Cramer, 4 Bn. Royal Munster Fusiliers.
　Temp. Lieut. D. G. T. K. Cross.
　2nd Lieut. S. F. L. Bell, 3 Bn. South Lancashire Regiment.
　2nd Lieut. V. M. Studd, 5 Bn. Rifle Brigade.
　2nd Lieut. T. B. C. Piggott, 4 Bn. Lancashire Fusiliers.
　Temp. Lt. E. L. Pearce.
　Temp. Lieut. C. W. Le Grand.
　2nd Lieut. (on prob.) J. H. Barrett, 3 Bn. Royal Lancashire Regi-
　　ment.
　2nd Lieut. C. W. H. Parker, Worcester Regiment.
　2nd Lieut. (on prob.) D. I. Grant, 3 Bn. Royal Inniskilling Fusiliers.
　2nd Lieut. P. S. Emerton, 4 Bn. Royal Warwickshire Regiment.
　2nd Lieut. (on prob.) C. C. R. Lacon, 4 Bn. Royal Warwickshire
　　Regiment.

Quarter-Masters

1 Lieut. P. T. Easton, Reserve of Officers.
2 2nd Lieut. T. G. Beeton, Unattached List (T.F.).
3 Qr.-Mr. and Hon. Lieut. B. G. Cavanagh, 6 Bn. London Rifles.

GOLD COAST REGIMENT

Lieut. Colonel

Capt. R. A. De B. Rose, Worcester Regiment.

Major

Capt. P. E. L. Elgee, Royal Berkshire Regiment.

ARTILLERY

Captain

Capt. N. L. St. Clair, Royal Artillery.

INFANTRY

Captains

Capt. H. Goodwin, Middlesex Regiment.
Capt. C. G. Hornby, East Lancashire Regiment, Adjt.
Capt. A. E. O'Meara, Manchester Regiment.
Lieut. G. Shaw, South Lancashire Regiment.
Capt. H. I. E. Ripley, Worcester Regiment.
Capt. B. V. Ramsden, Yorkshire Regiment.
Capt. J. H. Pelly, Worcester Regiment.
Capt. J. F. P. Butler, King's Royal Rifle Corps.
Capt. D. H. Magee, Yorkshire Regiment.

Lieutenants

Capt. J. H. Ratton, Royal Artillery.
Capt. W. A. Simpson, Royal Artillery.
Capt. R. H. Poyntz, Shropshire Light Infantry.
Capt. H. B. Dawes, Bedfordshire Regiment.
Capt. E. G. Wheeler, Hampshire Regiment.
Capt. J. L. Leslie-Smith, Border Regiment.
Capt. H. Read, Canadian Militia., Paymr. and Qr.-Mr.
Lieut. J. V. Earle, Notts and Derby Regiment.
Lieut. N. K. Steuart, Connaught Rangers.
Lieut. A. I. Macpherson, Suffolk Regiment.
Lieut. H. R. Greene, Hampshire Regiment.
Lieut. A. W. H. Baker, North Staffordshire Regiment.
2nd Lieut. E. Denwood, Worcester Regiment.

SIERRA LEONE BATTALION

Lieut. Colonel.

Capt. W. C. N. Hastings, D.S.O., Manchester Regiment.

Majors

Capt. R. E. H. Lockley, Gordon Highlanders.
Capt. F. Anderson, Royal Scots.

Captains

Capt. H. R. Ayton, Royal Artillery.
Capt. L. d'A. Fox, Royal Welch Fusiliers.
Capt. F. H. Hawley, West Yorkshire Regiment.
Capt. J. F. Drake, East Surrey Regiment.
Capt. A. N. Ogilvie, North Stafford Regiment.

Lieutenants

Capt. L. D. Gordon-Alexander, West Yorkshire Regiment.
Capt. G. E. R. de Miremont, Royal Welch Fusiliers.
Capt. H. T. Horsford, Gloucester Regiment (L.)
Capt. W. A. Campbell, North Lancashire Regiment.
Capt. II. II. Beattie, Northumberland Regiment.
Capt. M. J. Parker, South Staffordshire Regiment.
Capt. H. S. Finch, Lancashire Regiment, *Adjt.*
Capt. A. B. Thomson, East Kent Regiment.
Capt. R. Law, Royal Dublin Fusiliers.
Lieut. G. Dawes, South Staffordshire Regiment.
Lieut. C. D. Acheson, Royal Scots.
Lieut. G. S. Clements, Royal Irish Rifles.
Temp. 2nd Lieut. C. Baldwin, 11 (Serv.) Bn., Gloucester Regiment.

GAMBIA COMPANY

Captain Commanding

Capt. V. B. Thurston, Dorsetshire Regiment.

Lieutenants

Capt. A. McC. Inglis, Gloucester Regiment.
Capt. H. G. V. M. Freeman, Cheshire Regiment.

APPENDIX IV

FIRST ORDER OF BATTLE OF THE
ANGLO-FRENCH EXPEDITIONARY FORCE AGAINST
THE CAMEROONS
23rd September, 1914

GENERAL HEADQUARTERS

General Officer Commanding : Brig. General C. M. Dobell.[1]
A.D.C. : Lieut. G. E. R. de Miremont.[5]
Chief of Staff : Lieut. Col. A. J. Turner.[1]
General Staff Officer : Major J. Brough.[1]
French Officer attached : Captain A. Charvet.[2]
Deputy Assistant Adjutant and Quartermaster General : Capt. R. H. Rowe.[1]
Director of Signals : Capt. F. L. N. Giles, R.E.[1]
Director of Medical Services : Major J. C. B. Statham, R.A.M.C.[2]
Chief Supply and Transport Officer : Capt. D. A. Wallbach.[3][5]
Financial Officer : Mr. H. St. J. Sheppard.[1]
Political Officer : Mr. K. V. Elphinstone.[1]
Intelligence Officer : Lieut. D. McCallum.[1]

GENERAL HEADQUARTERS TROOPS

Camp Commandant : Lieut. A. McC. Inglis (Gambia Company, W.A.F.F.).
Headquarters escort : 25 rank and file, Gold Coast Regiment.
Signal Company : 2 British N.C.O.'s, 20 native ranks (from Gambia Company and Nigeria Regiment).
Royal Engineers : (*Capt. P. J. Mackesy, R.E.*)[4] Railway Section—Lieut. H. E. Kentish, R.E., 10 Europeans and 7 natives. Telegraph Section—Mr. H. M. Woolley, 6 Europeans and 12 natives. Field Section—Lieut. C. V. S. Jackson, R.E., 1 British N.C.O. and 13 natives (from 36th Company R.E. at Sierra Leone).

---

[1] Sailed from England in s.s. *Appam*.
[2] Joined the *Appam* at Sierra Leone.
[3] From the Nigerian Service. He had fought at Tel el Kebir in 1882 as a corporal.
[4] The Royal Engineers included Ex-R.E. officers and N.C.O.'s employed in Nigeria and the Gold Coast, and civilians from the Public Works, Railway and Telegraph Departments.
[5] Joined *Appam* at Lagos.

BRITISH CONTINGENT

BRITISH CONTINGENT HEADQUARTERS

Officer Commanding : Col. E. H. Gorges.
Second-in-Command : Lt. Col. F. H. G. Cunliffe.
General Staff Officer : Major W. D. Wright.
Attached General Staff : Captain H. G. Howell.
Staff Captain : Capt. C. R. U. Savile.
Staff Capain (attached) : Capt. C H. Dinnen.
Senior Medical Officer : Major W. H. G. H. Best (R.A.M.C. Special Reserve).
Ordnance Officer : Major H. W. G. Meyer-Criffith.

HEADQUARTERS TROOPS

Pioneer Company, Gold Coast Regiment (Capt. H. Goodwin), 5 officers, 2 British N.C.O.'s, 149 native ranks.

ARTILLERY

Sierra Leone Company, R.G.A. (Capt. N. d'A. Fitzgerald) : 4 2.95″ guns, 3 officers, 2 British N.C.O.'s, 46 native ranks.
No. 1 Battery, Nigeria Regiment (Capt. C. F. S. Maclaverty) : 4 2.95″ guns, 3 officers, 2 British N.C.O.'s, 64 native ranks.
Section, Gold Coast Battery (Lieut. W. L. St. Clair) : 2 2.95″ guns, 2 officers, 1 British N.C.O., 28 native ranks.

INFANTRY

West African Regiment (Lieut. Col. E. Vaughan) : 6 companies, 23 officers, 18 British N.C.O.'s, 643 native ranks.
No. 1 Battalion, Nigeria Regiment (Lieut. Col. J. B. Cockburn) : 4 companies (" A " and " F " Companies 1st Bn., " D " and " F " Companies, 2nd Bn. Nigeria Regiment), 28 officers, 12 British N.C.O.'s, 620 native ranks.
No. 2 Battalion, Nigeria Regiment (Lieut. Col. A. H. W. Haywood) : 4 companies (" A," " D," " E " and " F " Companies, 4th Bn. Nigeria Regiment), 21 officers, 12 British N.C.O.'s, 600 native ranks.
Composite Battalion (Lieut. Col. R. A. de B. Rose) : 4 companies— Two companies (" C " and " E ") Sierra Leone Battalion, W.A.F.F. (14 officers, 6 British N.C.O.'s, 211 native ranks).
Two companies (" B " and " F ") Gold Coast Regiment (which did not join the force till 25th September, 1914).

MEDICAL

19 officers, 4 British N.C.O.'s, 20 natives.

SUPPLY AND TRANSPORT (Lieut. G. F. Hodgson)

13 officers, 1 British N.C.O., 10 native superintendents and headmen, 3553 carriers.

Total

154 officers.
81 British N.C.O.'s and other European personnel.
2460 native ranks.
3563 carriers.
10 guns (2.95").

FRENCH CONTINGENT

HEADQUARTERS

Officer Commanding : Col. Mayer. Four staff officers, and Capt. H. T. Horsford attached as British liaison officer.

ARTILLERY

One mountain battery (Capt. Gerrard) : 6 guns.

INFANTRY

One company European Colonial Infantry (Capt. Salvetat) : 155 of all ranks.
No. 1 Senegalese Battalion (Commandant Mechet) : 4 companies, 18 officers, 44 French N.C.O.'s, 844 native ranks.
No. 2 Senegalese Battalion (Commandant Mathieu) : 4 companies, 15 officers, 51 French N.C.O.'s, 854 native ranks.

ENGINEERS (one section)

1 officer, 9 Europeans, 20 native ranks.
Medical, ammunition and transport details.

Total

54 officers.
354 European N.C.O.'s and men.
1859 native ranks.
1000 carriers.
200 animals (of which 75 were battery mules and the remainder horses).

INDEX

A

Adams, Lieutenant (R.N.), 129
Anderson, Major F., 254
Armitage, Captain C. H., 56
Atkin, Lieut. Col. B. G., 45, 221, 222, 232
Aymerich, General, French Commandant, 205, 207, 210, 216, 218, 219, 225, 230, 231, 256, 257, 264

B

Barker, Captain, 53
Beaty-Pownall, Captain C. P. (R.N.), 88, 135
Bennet, Lieutenant, R. D., 166
Biddulph, Captain L. S., 193, 234
Bird, Major M. H. C., 40
Bismarck, Prince von, 60, 152
Blum, Captain, 230
Bonham, Major C. B., 40
Booth, Major, 256
Bouchez, Captain, 56
Bowyer-Smijth, Captain C. G., 239
Braithwaite, Commander L. W., 168, 171
Brand, Captain E. S., 46, 147, 166
Brisset, Colonel (French officer), 207, 211, 215, 216, 229, 230, 256, 257
Bryant, Colonel F. C., 53, 57
Burt, Captain C. S. S., 45, 250, 251
Butler, Captain J. F. P., 193, 235, 236

C

Campbell, Governor, 27
Carré, Capitaine de Vaisseau, 263
Carter, Colonel C. H. P. 79, 83, 131
Cary, Lieutenant A. J. L., 224
Castaing, Captain (French officer), 54
Cavendish, Thomas, 24
Chamley, Captain J. W., 182, 184
Childs, Captain H. A. (R.N.), 102, 170
Clifford, Sir Hugh, 53
Cockburn, Lieut. Col. J. B., 146, 163–165, 172, 173, 194, 195, 200, 201, 234, 235
Cole, Brevet-Major S. J., 234
Cotton, Lieut. Col., 228, 229, 240, 250
Crailsheim, Hauptmann von, 212
Croft, Colour-Sergeant R., 204
Crookenden, Major, 228–230, 240, 241, 245, 246
Cunliffe, Brigadier-General F. J., 96, 133, 146, 148, 207, 208, 210, 212–216, 223–226, 228, 229, 238, 240, 253, 256, 259, 264

D

Dakeyne, Lieut. Col. H. W., 46
Dalrymple-Hamilton, Lieutenant (R.N.), 124
Daniell, Major General Sir John 36, 40, 134
Denham, Governor, 27

281